The Clairvoyance Handbook
A Practical Guide to Mediumship

A. L. Hale

The author of this book does not dispense medical advice or prescribe the use of any techniques as a form of treatment for physical or mental problems without the advice of a general practitioner/physician, either directly or indirectly. The intent of the author is only to offer information of a general nature to help you in your quest for emotional and spiritual wellbeing. In the event that you use any of the information in this book for yourself, which is your constitutional right, the author and publisher assume no responsibility for your actions.

This book is dedicated to

my Dad,

John James Obermaier.

The instigator of my spiritual journey,

who went back home on 12th January 2009.

Until We Meet Again.

A special thanks to my wonderful husband

for his completely endless support,

and to my family for not ordering a padded room

and strait-jacket!

"Don't fear failure so much that you refuse to try new things. The saddest summary of life contains three descriptions: could have, might have, and should have."

Louise E. Boone

CONTENTS

Introduction – May Contain Nuts!

Do forgive my opening words to you, but after years of thinking that I was the most sceptical person on the planet, who never believed in anything spiritual, I find it quite funny that I'm here talking to you about learning how to be spiritual. I don't claim to have all the answers, but I can certainly tell you about my own experiences of learning and describe the exercises that I practiced whilst in a development circle, lead by a brilliant clairvoyant.

I admit I was always fascinated by the way clairvoyants worked and how they claimed to have seen or heard things from a very young age. I knew that I had never seen any deceased relatives sitting on the end of my bed or heard them talking to me, so I therefore assumed that I didn't have the 'ability' to communicate with those who had passed on. This was something that I believed up until my late thirties. I was one of those typical cynics that thought that most spiritual readings were fabulous guesswork and pretty ambiguous all in all, with the occasional one that was genuine. I had been to a Tarot reading once at a psychic fair and found the whole thing very woolly and I was not at all convinced about the clairvoyant's abilities. I was due to travel – yes I go on holiday each year! I would marry once for life – I was then living with a boyfriend, but I am currently on my MKII husband. I had been away recently (the tan lines were pretty evident) and there was a stern-looking woman who had passed over sending her love – you could take your pick of *any* of my female relatives who had passed over.

I began my spiritual development in my late thirties after my father passed away. We had always had a difficult relationship from when I was around 10 years old. Our lives were completely different to one another's and as a consequence we found it hard to bond. At the time that he passed, I was running a business with my husband. We enjoyed working hard and playing hard too, with annual holidays and the odd weekend away. We had a nice home, two happy boys, a scruffy yet cute mutt and a very miserable cat. My Dad, on the other hand, lived in a council flat, spent as much time as possible drinking with his friends in the local Working Men's Club and never had a penny to spend. We were literally worlds apart, and despite us both wanting to bridge the gap between us, we never did. When he died in 2009, it completely blew the wind out of my sails. I found myself devastated, which I never anticipated as we had not been close. I felt guilty for not doing more for him; I was desperate to tell him that I was sorry and that I loved him dearly. I really didn't know which way to turn and, despite my family supporting me, I felt the only way to make the pain go away was to tell him how I felt. Having contact with him was obviously going to be a bit problematic as his ashes were scattered at sea, so conversations with each other were a little one- sided.

I found myself grieving for the relationship we should have had and I was anxious to tell him how I felt. This only really left me one option, which was to speak to a medium that could pass my message on to him and who would hopefully give me a message in return. The problem was that I didn't believe in most clairvoyants and I wanted to speak to someone who could prove to me my Dad was in spirit. After much reading and researching, I finally found one. It was after I had my first ever reading that my own spiritual journey started. It was quite slow to begin with, but the real change came for me after joining a development circle. A medium taught us weekly skills that we could practise in a relaxed and easy to follow way. The effect was incredible, as for the first time I was being taught to follow my natural instincts, to use what felt right to me rather than what I thought I should be doing. Once I started practising what I had learnt, my development began to race along and I was soon feeling more confident as the weeks went past.

I discovered that we are all born with the ability to communicate with spirit. It's not something that only a few special people can do. You categorically do *not* have to have Native American or Romany gypsy blood flowing through your veins. You do not have to be a regular church goer or part of a tree hugging circle. You do not need to believe in witchcraft, wear black clothing, or spend most of your time in the presence of cats. Any person of any age, intellect, or religion, has the ability. They just need to believe it and know what to look for. It's the one aspect that many people struggle with and the one fact that some people flatly refuse to believe. We have been raised to believe in predominately scientifically proven facts and evidence, therefore mediumship requires a deep belief and faith. We rely so much on technology which is progressing at an immense rate and dismissing the skills that we are inherently born with.

Most Western societies do not easily embrace a spiritual upbringing. Although most children are at their most receptive to seeing and sensing spirits at a young age, we teach them to block out any communications they may have with the spirit world. This is mainly because we think we are protecting our children and we are afraid of what we ourselves cannot see or explain. How many stories do you hear of children speaking or talking to imaginary friends, or seeing relatives that have passed on? Look at it from the other side. Would you want to keep in contact with your grandchildren after you pass on? If they could see and hear you, don't you think that you would want to say hello? In the same way in which we long to speak to our loved ones once they have passed on, to hear that they are safe and with other family members in spirit, they also want to communicate and reassure us, too.

Once we have accepted the fact that spirits are all around us and that they want to work with us, probably as much as we want to work with them, the rest will become easier. What you need to have is patience and belief. You also need to make time to communicate with spirit. You were not born being able to read; it was a skill you had to learn and practise. Mediumship is the same and you can also learn to communicate with those in spirit. With practise and patience it gets easier and your messages will come through more clearly. You will no longer believe it's your imagination. It will also give you the reassurance that death is certainly not the end for our loved ones, but just the beginning of a new journey. As someone once said to me, 'You have more to fear from the living than you do the dead' and once you have learnt to develop your skills, you will be able to tune in to the spirit world when and how you choose to.

I have written this book as a guide, as I personally struggled to find anything written down from a learner's point of view and felt that it would be helpful to share my failings and successes with you. After all there is something quite comforting about knowing that other people have completely stuffed things up and felt like a twit, too! When I was in my early stages of learning, I wanted someone to explain to me why I found some parts of mediumship difficult and others parts easy. I wanted to read about all of the typical stumbling blocks and anxieties that others practising mediumship went through whilst they were learning. I wanted easy to follow exercises that didn't involve banging gongs and chanting for hours. So hopefully this book will make learning easier and more effective for you. It answers many of the questions which most people ask when they are learning. It describes my own journey too, with all of the highs and lows that I felt along the way and explains various simple methods for developing your own mediumship. Trust me, you're not nuts, you're just starting to look at things a little differently.

A little about me...

I wanted to include a piece about how my spiritual journey and how it began. This is to show you that you really can begin at any age, without any previous practice. As mentioned earlier, I had no prior experience of becoming a clairvoyant or developing a psychic ability, in fact far from it. My Dad separated from my Mum when I was 10 years old, to live with a woman who was 13 years his junior. The relationship didn't last long and soon after they, too, separated, once the novelty had worn thin for her. He moved into a small flat on his own and it was not long after that he turned to drink and started to borrow money from me. His health was never very good, due to asthma and emphysema and the alcohol only exacerbated matters. At this point I had only noticed a little contact from the spirit world when I had some unexplained experiences as a teenager. The incidents scared me out of my wits, so much so that from then on I wanted to shut anything connected to the spirit world out of my life. The rest of my early years were troubled, to put it delicately, due to an abusive man who did his utmost to control both my Mum and I. Consequently I left home to rent a bedsit when I reached sixteen and found work at weekends. I could not bear to watch my Mum's self-esteem washing away and although her physical bruises healed, the mental ones took their toll heavily on both of us for years after.

I soon found full-time work as an administrative officer and not long after I settled down to become a wife and mother at a young 21 years. I had two beautiful boys who were both born with a form of autism called Asperger's Syndrome. Sometimes life was difficult but we coped well and the years passed quickly. I divorced amicably in 2002 and not long after I decided that it was about time to do something for myself, so I went to college in the same year. I found college to be quite difficult in the beginning. Being a single parent of two children with learning disabilities was a struggle in itself, added to the fact that it had been some years since I last sat in a classroom. I muddled through and threw myself fully into education, eventually progressing further and finally going on to university. I trained to become a nurse and in 2005 I qualified and met a new man. We soon settled down with each other and we married in 2007. Life was busy in the usual way that all parents can identify with and everything was suitably 'normal' in a chaotic sort of way. My new husband was an incredibly creative chap who undertook graphic design and theming, but needed someone to handle his accounts and be a general admin slave. After some deliberation I decided to give up my nursing job, which was in a young offender's prison at that point and take up the position of financial director of the business.

My life changed dramatically at the beginning of 2009, and it was the following chain of events that resulted in the start of my whole spiritual journey. At the beginning of January 2009, I had been the financial director of the business for a year and found that work was reaching our busiest time. I had seen my father the day before New Year's Eve and spent some time with him. To say my Dad and I had a strained relationship would be reasonably accurate. He was a very kind hearted man and would be very generous, but unfortunately he was dependent on alcohol. He also lived quite a lonely life on the whole, despite being surrounded by drinking buddies. I saw him on that day for a while, then had a phone call from him a few days later on Saturday 4th January. He said that he had developed bronchitis and although he had been given antibiotics he was struggling to breathe. I immediately called an ambulance for him and he was taken to hospital straight away. Over the years he'd had numerous hospital visits due to such poor health, so I didn't think anything untoward would happen on this occasion. With my nurse's hat on, I thought that with IV antibiotics, good nutrition and no alcohol to drink, that his body would soon recover.

A few days later I phoned the hospital to see how he was and ended up speaking to a consultant. The consultant asked me to come straight in to the hospital as soon as I could. Having been a nurse for some years, I knew this was not a good sign. I was fully aware of the consequences of his illness and I suddenly became painfully conscious that things were about to get a lot worse. Despite all my years of medical training, I found myself for the first time being unable to help him. My Dad's breathing had become incredibly laboured over the weekend and had developed into pneumonia. He had been taken to intensive care and when I saw him he was being ventilated by a machine. He was completely unconscious and I was quite shocked to see him so ill. The consultant explained to me that a fit and healthy person would take months to recover from pneumonia. He said that if my father came off the ventilator, he had less than a one in three chance of surviving. He asked what I wanted to do as he could not remain ventilated indefinitely. I recall crying so much, knowing that the consultant was asking my permission to take him off of the ventilator. It was a horrible decision to have to make. He said that he felt my Dad's quality of life was so poor due to his bad health that it would be the kindest thing not to resuscitate him should his heart stop. He said it would be better to make him as comfortable as possible if this happened. After some thought, I tentatively agreed.

His body had already started shutting down before he was taken to intensive care. It was in such a poor state that I had a strong feeling that once off the ventilator he would not survive long. He was due to come off the ventilator in the following days after seeing the consultant and over that time I went to see him, even though he was unconscious. On one of the journeys up to the hospital, I remember crying and praying that if he was going to die soon could I please have a sign, as I was so upset by not knowing if he would pull through. I saw no less than five funeral cars carrying coffins on that journey so, sadly, I had got my answer.

On the Thursday, the day in which his breathing tubes were being removed, I had arranged to go up and see him but kept having excruciating pains in my stomach. As a result, I never made it in to see him. That night, I was taken into the same hospital with a large ovarian cyst that was about to burst. The irony of being in the same hospital was almost comical. For the next two days the nurses would wheel me down the corridor to see my Dad; I would be dressed in my fluffy dressing gown and pink happy pig slippers that my husband had bought for me to make me smile! As Dad came off the ventilator, he quite unexpectedly became conscious again, but was struggling to breathe. For a brief time I held his hand and spoke to him; although he was not very lucid he did realise that I was unwell and asked why I was in hospital in my nightie. I told him that I had 'women' problems, but that it was nothing to worry about and that I'd be fine. We hugged and said that we loved each other, but I knew that he didn't have long left in this world.

One of the nurses was particularly rough with my father and also happened to be someone I had trained with at university. We had never got along very well and I was not happy that she had little time for him. I was told by my Dad's consultant one night, when she came down to the ward to visit me, that Dad would flatly refuse to let this nurse touch him and that he would not even let her near him at all. The consultant also told me that when Dad had spoken to her earlier, he had said that he knew he was dying and asked if she would please just let him go. At the time they were carrying out observations on him frequently, which he absolutely hated. He was dying and he knew it. He wanted to be left alone without any needles or nurses to bother him. Having spoken to the consultant, it was decided to move my Dad to a quiet side-room on a different ward and all invasive observations were stopped. I called all of his friends and family to explain that he had just days left to live and, those who could, came up to say goodbye. It was the most difficult and saddening time I had ever experienced.

On the Saturday morning I decided to discharge myself, as the cyst had finally burst and the pain was slowly diminishing. I went back to see Dad later that day and spoke with him, saying that I would be back first thing the next day. I had a phone call in the early hours of the morning however, at about 2.30am, saying that it may be a good idea to come in to hospital as Dad was losing his fight for life. For the next 22 hours he fought on; I held his hand constantly and talked to him the whole time. I told him how much I loved him and that, despite our differences, he was still my Dad and I wished that things could have been different. I talked about my children, I talked about his childhood and the stories I remember him telling me, I talked about all of the good things we had done together. I talked and cried, and talked some more, not wanting to let go. The nurses came in around 9.30pm and suggested I go home to sleep for a while. They said that they would call me if there was any change again. At just after midnight the nurse called to say that Dad had passed away and I felt my world crumble; I simply wanted him back.

My husband and I made the journey together, on a cold, snowy January night, to see him for what I believed to be the last time. Seeing his empty and broken body was very hard, but in some ways it helped because it was exactly that, empty - there was no part of him in pain. He looked very pale, but like he was asleep, and I remember hugging him and holding his hand, willing him to come back even for a minute. My tears flowed and flowed in a stream of grief and although I knew he had gone and was finally at peace, it still felt wrong.

The next days were achingly painful and when I went to register the death, I was by myself and feeling awful. Sitting in the waiting room alone, which happened to be one of the most oppressive places I had been in for some time, I struggled not to cry. In that moment, I had the feeling of my Dad sitting next to me. I can't explain how, but I absolutely knew he was with me and he continued to sit with me until I was called through by the registrar. It was a very odd but comforting moment and I didn't want to tell anyone about it at first. I thought they would think I was being over emotional and say that it was my imagination, so I kept quiet. The weeks slowly passed by and every day was tough; the ache left within me was almost palpable. I had frequently heard people say that it physically hurts to lose someone, and had never realised what they meant. After losing my own Dad, I can honestly say that I knew exactly what they meant.

I felt other people's reactions to be a very odd experience because they literally didn't know what to say and would often avoid me. They didn't want to ask how I was, for fear of turning me into an emotional blubbing wreck. It's not they didn't care; they just didn't know how I was going to behave and were scared of my possible reaction. Again, this was something I had not experienced before; I found it quite strange, because I *did* want to talk about it even if they didn't. In the first week or so most people said they were sorry to hear of my sad news and some would ask how I was. After that it was as though most people expected me to carry on as normal, which I did, after a fashion, but with a large dark cloud following me. I would often find myself welling up with tears at the oddest moments; shopping for groceries for instance and finding items that I knew my Dad would have loved to eat, or bits and bobs that he often bought for himself. I remember talking to someone about it and saying that if I just knew that he was okay, then I would feel better. When she suggested I consult a medium, I didn't think too much about it at the time, but as the days went by I thought about it more and more. I found myself researching people on the internet who were recommended. I came across a chap, Paul Derrick, who was a fireman and also a medium. I got in contact by e-mail and he seemed very friendly and approachable. We arranged a time and date for me to call him for a phone reading. I was very doubtful about how Paul would communicate with my Dad. I thought it would be difficult to read for me over the phone, without seeing me in person. I thought Paul would need something to go on, such as a photograph of my Dad or a personal possession of his, but he assured me this was not necessary. He explained to me that although we were about 70 miles away from each other, he could still do a reading, and if I was happy with it, then I would pay him after. This sounded like a good deal to me. It would be an excellent way of this medium proving his skills, particularly as he could not see me, or read my body language.

Dad Says Hi

That evening before I called Paul, I spent half an hour in my bedroom with photos of my Dad, and I made sure I was as relaxed as I could be. I called Paul who explained how the process would work. He could only pass on the messages that he received and I was to answer only by saying 'Yes, no or don't know'. I was to give no other information unless asked to explain something. Straight away he felt the presence of a male who had passed with terrible breathing troubles and I hoped that my Dad had come though.

Paul went on and told me things that I had said to my Dad the night he passed away, things that only I knew of. He spoke of 'that bloody nurse', who was rough with him. He described the room I was sitting in at that time, right down to the furniture. His message was so accurate, it was incredible. He talked about our relationship being strained and how Dad wanted to tell me that it was his time to pass on. Dad also apologised 'for being a pain in the arse'- one of his most used phrases- and I sat there almost stunned by Paul's words. Dad said that I had made the right decision as he had been ready to go. My Dad was very happy and at peace where he was. His legs and breathing were fantastic again and although we hadn't had a close relationship before he passed, he was very much with me now. In fact he had so much love, if he could hug me he would not let go easily and he was sorry that we never did build those bridges whilst he was alive. Paul told me of things that were going to happen in the near future that I had no idea about, all of which did happen. He also told me that every so often I had felt my Dad's presence with me, but later doubted those feelings. At that point I suddenly felt an incredible tingling sensation on the top left side of my head; a little like when you rub a balloon on your head, but more intense. Paul then said to me, 'You know that feeling you have just had, your Dad says that is him, he is with you.' It was unbelievable, predominantly because we were on the phone and he could not see me at all.

His reading gave me such comfort that I could not thank him enough. I knew beyond all doubt my Dad had come through and was with me. I cannot describe it easily, but I had an immense feeling of him being at peace. In one evening I felt my Dad had said more to me about our relationship with each other than he ever had before. I finally felt that we had built the bridges that we should have built years ago. To this day I am grateful for the messages Paul gave to me, as they finally helped me to move on.

For days after my head was reeling with questions about how Paul had done this. I didn't believe it to be guesswork as it was far too accurate, but I did want to know how he had received his information. I spent weeks researching clairvoyance as, being quite a grounded, realistic person, I wanted to learn more about this gift people had. I wanted to know if this gift was a skill that could be learned. I remember thinking that if I could feel such comfort from such a skill, then surely other people would benefit from it, too. If a reading was as accurate as mine had been, then surely there would be little doubt that there must be an afterlife.

From that point on I began reading books about life after death and how death is very much the beginning of a new journey. I read about how some mediums worked and how they all said that they learned to trust the messages and information they received over time. Most noticed their gift at a young age and were confident in their ability as adults. Some had tried to block out spirit contact initially, but in the end they had learned to work with it. This was not the case with me however, as I had only had little contact from spirit and so I continued to research more. I became fascinated with clairvoyance and started to read further books about how mediums had developed their ability. Most I felt were too 'spiritual' for me at that point in my life; several talked about different levels of angels, spirit guides, unblocking and aligning chakras, low level entities, rules and systems, all of which seemed a lot to take in and I felt the books were too advanced for me. I wanted to develop naturally and was not interested in knowing every minuscule detail about rules, how to chant to angels and the hierarchy of light beings. They did, however, all mention the same thing - that trusting your instincts is the key and to practise as is necessary in learning any new skills.

I don't want to criticise what other writers have written about developing mediumship skills, far from it. For some people, reading lots of factual information will suit them entirely. They may develop their skills perfectly well using books with lots of information and facts. What I will say is that for me personally, this was not the case. I wanted to follow someone's journey from a novice's perspective, and have the chance to read about the typical mistakes, anxieties and doubts that most people must go through whilst they learn. For me the early stages were a matter of using my instincts more, some things just felt right. It was that sort of knowing when, for example, the phone rings and you just know who it's going to be. Yes, it could be a lucky guess, but deep down you just somehow know you are right and it was those instinctive feelings that I continued to work on.

Around 2009, my husband and I took another leap of faith and decided to close the business to work on a new project. This was something my husband had wanted to do for years and years. So eventually we decided to take the plunge, to close our existing business and run with something new. In order to do this I knew that he would not make enough money in the early days, so I decided that I wanted to teach nursing. The same month that I made this decision, a teaching post came up at my local college. They wanted someone to teach health & social care, preferably with a medical background and also be able to assess the students in their work environment. It seemed almost too perfect and I felt that this job had almost been put my way. A year later I had a teaching qualification and I loved my job immensely. I was able to put all of my experience of nursing together with my experience of learning disabilities and teaching. As a result, my students blossomed.

They were all mature students who were mostly unsure of their abilities to pass the course. It was quite an intensive and academic course, which, when you have not been in a classroom for some years, is very daunting. Over the months, though, I watched their confidence grow and they all flourished with my encouragement. I had total faith that they all had the ability to succeed as long as they continued to work at it. Every one of them passed their course and I still keep in contact with many from my first class. They all worked so hard, despite their nerves, and more importantly they proved to themselves that they could all succeed.

During this time I practised meditating and found that just before I fell asleep I would hear voices, or random snippets of conversation. They were from people young and old, with different accents, talking about all sorts of subjects, none of which meant a thing to me. It was like trying to tune into a specific radio channel and getting several different ones instead! When I say hear voices, I would hear them in my head, not out loud. For example, if I said to you to imagine a Scottish man around 30 years of age, talking to you about his house, I expect you to imagine what he would sound like. This was what it was like for me, except that I would 'hear' snippets of conversation in my head that were not my own thoughts. I find even now that I am most 'tuned in' last thing at night and first thing in the morning when I am most relaxed, but through meditating I can achieve a similar state. I will go into more detail about how I get into a meditative state later and you can try this for yourself.

I also began to 'feel' spirits around me, and this became more prevalent over time. I would literally get the feeling of being 'plugged in', experiencing the most incredible tingling sensation in my head- usually on the left side- accompanied by the feeling that someone was with me. I discovered, over time, that I could identify if the person was male or female and I would also sense emotions felt by that person. I have since found that just because a person is not with us in body anymore, it does not mean that they do not feel emotions still. People who have passed still feel joy, love and happiness along with remorse, sadness and guilt, just the same as we do.

One of my biggest worries when starting out was that my family and friends would think I was completely mad. I could almost hear the conversations at the family Christmas party, "Allow me to introduce you to Amy, she is the financial director of a business and thinks she speaks to dead people,"- not quite the image I was hoping for! All I can say is that, yes, you are *always* going to come up against a sceptic. Crikey, I should know – I used to be one of them! It's incredibly hard not to feel embarrassed or awkward in certain situations when your 'gift' is mentioned. However, in the same way that you want to surround your children with only the 'nice' boys and girls from school, who accept your child regardless of their idiosyncrasies, you also need to do the same for yourself. Surround yourself with people who support you, even if they do not understand what you are trying to do. You do not have to tell someone about your ability if you don't want to, or you can do it when you are ready. The more you embrace your spiritual self, the more you will get back from the spirit world in return.

In 2011, after much reading and practise, I felt that I wanted to develop what I was feeling and confirm that the messages I was receiving were accurate. During this time I found that, when in the company of someone I had never met, I could sense lots of information about them. I knew intuitively facts about them and their lives, which I later would discover were accurate. When I came across an advert for clairvoyant and psychic development classes in my area, I felt that this was absolutely the right time for me and decided to go along. I was incredibly nervous and really didn't know what to expect, but it was the breakthrough that I had been waiting for. My mediumship and psychic skills developed quite rapidly after only a few months. Towards the end of 2011, I felt it was time to find my own wings and help others to learn in the same way as I did, so I decided to write the book you have in front of you now. This was finally finished on 8th February, my Dad's birthday. It's certainly been an interesting journey with plenty of highs and lows, but for me that is exactly what life is about. You cannot see the light without first experiencing the darkness. Not all things immediately make sense. You can only join up the dots when you look back.

<u>Okay, enough about me, let's talk about you</u>

So you've got this far, which is great! You are hopefully still intrigued enough to continue and maybe still a bit sceptical, which is not a bad thing. You will learn to question everything. The aim of the book is to go through each of the following chapters together, then explore in more detail some of the experiences you may have had after carrying out the exercises in the chapters. If I have convinced you to at least have an open mind and follow some of the exercises, then you will be well on the way to improving your own spiritual awareness. At the very least, you will have a better understanding of the spiritual world.

The aim of this book is not to preach to you. Nor will it go into huge amounts of depth about the cosmos and all things spiritual that will leave your brain aching. I do not proclaim to have all of the answers, but I can certainly help direct you in a positive way that will enable you to develop your skills. If you are looking for an in depth book or one for of spiritual rituals, you are going to be disappointed, so please step away from the 'Buy' button.

The whole idea of each chapter is to trust what you feel and use what feels right for you! It's not a book crammed full of information about exercises and rituals you simply *must* follow. Just like learning a foreign language, you can get overwhelmed by the details and become bored very quickly. There is no point in learning all of the verbs and grammar behind a language, if all you are likely to want to learn is how to hold a basic conversation, such as, 'Where's the nearest pub and do they serve cold beer?' This is similar as it covers clairvoyance and psychic awareness in a wonderfully simple format. You will not get bogged down with stacks of information, as it should never feel like a chore to develop your skills. You will begin to get a feel of what works for you and what does not and it's good to know that we are all different. For me, I mostly hear messages (clairaudience) and feel emotions, other will see images (clairvoyance), some will prefer to use

Tarot cards, others photographs or possessions of those they are trying to connect with.

The main point to remember is that just because one person works in a particular way, it does not mean that you have to work in the same way. You have to trust what you feel and develop it. If you try to develop a skill that is not working for you, it will result in you losing your confidence, becoming frustrated and most likely giving up. You want to be able to use your skills accurately and give clear and concise readings. Stick with what's right for you and you will have more positive results and clearer readings.

I have found that most people who work as mediums, or those who are most 'sensitive', tend to have similar backgrounds. So if you can identify with the following aspects, then this may help you decide if you want to order the strait-jacket now, or wait until a bit further on.

Did you ever have an imaginary friend or animal?

Were you a quiet and reserved child?

Have you ever felt the presence of someone with you, when no-one was actually there?

Do you ever see vivid mental pictures, or hear inner voices?

Do crowded noisy places leave you feeling exhausted?

Do you often feel tired on waking, even after a good night's sleep?

Do you feel the atmosphere of a building when you walk in?

Have you felt that you are actually a strong person, despite being told that you are over- sensitive, irrational or emotional and imagining things that aren't really there?

Do you feel different, perhaps having some sense of not' belonging' in your family or environment?

You may have trouble remembering facts, but actually be very creative and imaginative.

Have you had a difficult childhood or troubled past?

If you can identify with several of the points above, I think you can safely assume that you have the right book in your hands. Remember that we learn in different ways, so dip your toes in by trying several methods and find out what seems successful to you. All mediums use techniques that feel right to them when communicating with the spirit world. There is no set routine that we all follow. Once you find the right method for you, your ability will begin to flourish. It is a case of trial and error in the early days, but I can assure you that we have all been there, it does get easier and you'll soon trust the information you receive.

"You were born with potential.
You were born with goodness and trust.
You were born with ideals and dreams.
You were born with greatness.
You were born with wings.
You are not meant for crawling, so don't.
You have wings...
Learn to use them and fly."

Rumi

Chapter 1: Claire Who?

There are different kinds of 'gifts', or abilities that most mediums and psychics seem to work with. Most of us use some sort of psychic ability every day, without even knowing it; we are more than likely picking up on information psychically all around us. Most people will prefer to call this ability something much more normal than psychic, such as 'using your intuition or instincts', which when boiled down will be exactly the same thing. How often do we hear people saying, 'I've just got a feeling that ... or I have a hunch that ...'? The odd thing about this is that when our hunches are accurate we openly brag about it to others, and say, 'See? I told you so'. Yet to say we are psychic is considered embarrassing. It's an ability commonly associated with women wearing huge head scarves, using crystal balls and advertising in the back of a newspaper. So why do we brag about our hunches or feelings in one breath, but are embarrassed by the word 'psychic' in the next? It is a word that most people find off putting, but try not to let this bother you. Your psychic ability will also develop as you learn more about the spirit world.

We know for a fact that we only use a fraction of our brain. How many of us, usually after a few glasses of wine or the odd beer or two, have sat down with our friends and debated how wonderful it would be to be able to use more than that fraction? We may even hypothesize over the wonders that we could achieve, *but* when it comes down to actually using our senses and opening our minds in a spiritual sense, we are usually ridiculed for doing so. It's a little like saying, 'Wouldn't it be fantastic if we could all talk to each other through the power of thought, but you wouldn't catch me attempting it, people will think I'm mad!' I am not suggesting that we can or will have this ability, but you can see where I am coming from. We let our egos take over and fear being ridiculed. This is one aspect which is really hard to overcome, but you do need to let go of the fear and accept that your ego may take a bit of knock here and there. So with that in mind, ignore the images that are stereotypically associated with the word psychic and see how you get on with the next part.

So what are these hunches and feelings we get?

Psychic – derives from the Greek word Psyche - meaning 'of the soul or of the mind, mental'. Quite apt really, as most people will think you are mental if you should use the word! This often makes it a less attractive skill to learn. It literally means using your senses to perceive information from a source that is outside of scientific or natural knowledge. So when you have that feeling that something is not quite right, or you just know that you are going to bump into someone you know, that is being psychic. It's often talked about in people who have a twin brother or sister. They have often felt that their twin is in pain or trouble; some quite literally feel the pain. This is not by using their usual senses, but instead they are tuning in to their twin's energy and can feel that something is causing them distress.

When you receive information from the spirit world, this comes in different forms. Although similar in some ways to a psychic ability, the one difference is that you are not getting your information from the 'living' world. Mediumship is a term that encompasses all forms of information that is received from the spirit world. All of the below terms are a form of mediumship.

Clairvoyance – derives from French origins 'Clair', meaning clear, and 'voyance' meaning vision. This is where you see events or images in your mind. Some people will see symbols or actual events and people. I find that when I am connecting to a person, or giving a reading, numerous images flash up from my own past at times. This is in addition to other images which I then interpret for the individual with me. For example, I have a photograph of my Dad's cherry red motorbike, so if I see this image in my mind, then I know the spirit I've connected to also had a connection with motorbikes. We also had an accident together on his motorbike when I was little, nothing serious thankfully, but again when I see this event in my head, then I know the spirit had a bike accident whilst alive. The key thing about clairvoyance is that you will see these images in your mind, not slap bang in front of you. I was taught to trust these images. For a long time I kept asking myself why I was seeing things from my past when I was reading for someone else. I thought I would be seeing things from their past, not mine. When Jody, a medium who ran the development circle, explained to the members that spirit will often work with our *own* memory bank and feelings, as well as giving us other images, I had one of those 'Eureka' moments. It suddenly made sense why I was seeing images of my own past when reading for someone else. I still see other images too; for example, I read for a lady and could clearly see her grandmother, complete with a walking frame and deep red, velvet, Velcro slippers. I don't see these images in front of me, instead I have thoughts and images that drop into my mind.

So imagine I asked you to picture a small cottage with a thatched roof somewhere in the countryside. An image should form in your mind of a cottage, complete with trees and a thatched roof. It won't necessarily be the same cottage as the one I visualise, but you should still be able to picture something fairly similar. Clairvoyance is the same. When I connect to someone I first get the impression of a male or female and the more I concentrate the more information I receive. I will start to see images and memories in my mind which will be related to the spirit I am in contact with.

Clairaudience – Yes you've got it, another word French in origin. This Clair refers to audience or hearing – literally 'clear hearing'. I wish it was that simple, though! Clear hearing was far from what I was getting when I was learning. In fact it was more like random conversations. I think this 'gift' is quite a difficult one to accept, as for a long time anyone who claims to hear voices has been declared to be anything from mad to schizophrenic. In my early stages I was hearing multiple voices, not talking directly to me though, but talking in general. It was as if I was listening in on telephone conversations and getting snippets here and there which had no relevance to me whatsoever. These voices were not heard as if someone was talking to me normally, but as if I were hearing thoughts. Over time, I was actually able to adjust the connection so they would be talking to me individually and it wasn't so random. The messages would again come in like thoughts; the main difference being that the thoughts were not mine. Eventually over time when completely relaxed, I began to actually 'hear' the voices, always just before I went to sleep each night. I would be in that in-between state of waking and sleeping, and my poor husband would find me suddenly sitting bolt upright in bed at night with my heart racing like a steam train, asking him if he had heard that voice. At first he was very concerned, as 'no' he had not heard anything and yet I was convinced that he must have done, because it was so loud. It was as if someone was talking right next to me. My husband is, thankfully, used to it now and I have learnt to control my reactions a little better. Although whilst asleep I am known to have long conversations with people! Having investigated this I have come across numerous people who have these experiences and it's referred to as hypnogogia. One account I read about made me chuckle because I could identify with it so well. It was from a respectable solicitor who was writing on a forum to ask if he was going mad, because he, too, was hearing voices before he went to sleep. He was too embarrassed to tell his family and his doctor had apparently been less than helpful. I am not sure if the forum gave any specific advice, but it was interesting to read the reactions of other people.

There is a wealth of information available about hypnogogia if you are interested. One that has most interested me was a very thorough account written by Andreas Mavromatis in his book, 'Hypnogogia: The Unique Stage of Consciousness Between Wakefulness and Asleep' (1987). He refers to man's spiritual vision and claims that it was originally provided by the third eye. He says that it was once available to everyone, but has now been temporarily lost. He felt that its return at a higher level is guaranteed through spiritual development and through use of hypnagogia. It is quite a deep read, so don't delve in until you are ready. Although most of his writing I can agree with, there are some bits that didn't quite fit well with me. There may be some bits I have written within this book that you feel just do not fit that well with you. It's completely up to you to decide what you take from this and what you don't. That's the whole purpose of it. It is written so that you can make an informed decision about what is right for you.

Clairsentient – If you think by stating this is another one of those French terms that you are using your psychic abilities, then I am afraid I cannot let you have this one! Clairsentient – yes, also French in origin is literally translated as 'clear feeling'. This is where you will feel emotions, possibly feel physical sensations, or smell aromas. Quite often when connecting to a spirit, a medium will feel the 'symptoms' that the spirit had. For example, every time my Dad comes through, most mediums instantly complain that they find it hard to breathe. Exactly in the same way as he did, they find their chests feel tight and that way I know it's him coming through. It can also refer to other aches and pains the spirit felt whilst alive; this is why some mediums start feeling similar aches or pains in that you become very aware of parts of your body. I quite often feel discomfort in my chest if a spirit died of a heart attack for example, or I often feel a little bump in my tummy that suddenly vanishes if a lady I'm reading for has suffered a miscarriage.

Every time I connect to spirit, I feel immense tingles down the back of my head. It's like someone has rubbed a balloon against something static and held it next to my head, a sort of gentle electrocution. The stronger the connection, the more 'tingles' I feel. In my early days I also found that I would feel quite nauseous and feel 'spaced out' when connecting to spirit, but now I don't get this at all. Different mediums feel different sensations, so don't get despondent if you don't experience the same feelings that I have described.

Most mediums tend to be sensitive to emotions and can feel the emotions of the spirit. Many spirits come through with messages of love, so when this happens to me I have this overwhelming feeling of happiness and love. Others come through with feelings of sadness or remorse, and again I experience those feelings. During my first ever reading that I gave, I sat with a lady and felt the same sensation I used to get after seeing my Dad when he was alive. I would come away from seeing him feeling frustrated and let down by his inability to change or motivate himself. I found myself having the same feelings again when doing this particular reading, which at the time was very odd. When I looked at this lady, I remember querying why on Earth I was thinking about my Dad and our relationship, when focusing on her? This was not a good time to be thinking about my past, when I was meant to be practising my clairvoyant skills, yet I couldn't shake off the feeling. It was only when I asked her if she'd had a poor relationship with her father that the penny dropped. Sure enough, they had had a very strained relationship; he had always been distant with her and she felt that he had sadly let her down. It suddenly made sense to me why I was having those emotions from my past. I then had an image of a man standing with his head held low in shame and he was saying sorry to her. It was then that I was able to establish that this man was her father who had passed on and I could actually feel his remorse. He was using my memory bank of feelings and emotions to deliver his message. It was very subtle and something I could have easily dismissed. I felt at the time that I was randomly thinking about my own Dad. This was a huge learning curve for me and I still tell myself even now to 'stop looking and start feeling!' When you get those feelings, they will mean something, even though they may be your own memories. You are unlikely to ever be having a full long conversation with a spirit. Instead, be aware that communication will be through using *all* of your senses. It's good to remember that you are extremely unlikely to see a fully blown apparition in front of you with a booming voice saying, 'Tell Jenny Dad sends his love, and by the way, she needs to get her car looked at.'

Messages that come though are very subtle and this is worth noting, particularly when you are starting out. You query absolutely everything and worry about making a complete twit of yourself in front of someone else. Many a week we would sit in our development circle looking at each other like we should be committed to a nearby asylum. We often felt awkward relaying the messages or feelings we were receiving, because it was so subtle we worried that we would get it wrong. When you start giving readings, you are so afraid of getting it inaccurate and seeing the person you are reading for looking back at you with a completely blank face. Getting it wrong can totally destroy your confidence and be quite deflating. However, do not panic!

During my first ever reading, I was given a message that I could not understand or relate to at all. The medium, Paul, started my reading by describing a bedroom to me, which was slightly unusual because the door was right in the middle of the wall on the inside, but did not look the same on the outside on the landing. It was joined to another room, creating an L shape. He described the double bed in the middle of the room, the mirror on the windowsill and other bits and pieces in the room, but nothing sounded familiar. I thought about every bedroom that my Dad had lived in and could not relate to what he was describing at all. I kept repeating 'no' to him. In the end Paul moved on and gave the rest of his reading, which was completely accurate. When I spoke to my husband about the reading and the bedroom that I could not identify, he started laughing. Paul had been describing the very room I had been sitting in at the time, but because I didn't understand how mediumship worked, I was too busy focusing on my Dad and where *he* had lived. It didn't even remotely occur to me that he would be able to 'see' the room I was in. I thought he would just see my Dad's life and not mine and be chatting merrily away to him. After the reading I was completely blown away by the amount of detail he used when describing my room, yet at the time I had told him that I had no idea what he was referring to. Paul described my Dad very clearly and told me things that only my Dad had said to me before he died, so I knew

Paul had my Dad with him. He was an established medium and had been doing his spiritual 'thing' for years and I had no doubts at all by the end of the reading. So just because the person you are reading for cannot identify or relate to part of a message, it doesn't necessarily mean it's wrong. It may instead be a case of them not being able to place your message at that time.

Once you start to dip your toes into the spiritual waters, you will find that you become more and more in tune to both spirits and people around you. You might find that your hunches are coming more frequently and that they are also more accurate. So to start you off on your journey, try to follow the exercises at the end of each chapter. If there is one that you do not particularly like, or do not find successful, then don't try to force it. Yes, you do need to practise, but if it does not feel right then don't beat yourself into practising a particular task. You will just end up becoming deflated and more than likely bored. If it feels right, you will know. You are just going to have to trust me on this one. If you are not sure how you feel about an exercise, then keep practising the exercise until you make a decision either way.

Exercise 1 – Tune in Your Psychic Channel

You will find that tuning in your psychic abilities, or for those of you who prefer something more normal sounding, sharpening your intuition, is something you can practise daily without anyone else knowing. Start by trying to predict something simple where you have a reasonable chance of getting it right. For example, when the phone rings, try to pick up on who is calling. Is it male or female? Is this someone you know well, or is it someone from your credit card company/bank giving you a 'courtesy call', or one of those annoying cold calls?

Another example to try is when you are in a queue at the bank, post-office, or similar place, where you can try to predict which person will serve you. If you have children, you can use this as a game and get them to 'play' with you. Are you drawn to any one person? Being drawn to a person because they're really good looking, or have a large wart, is not being intuitive!

One of my favourite exercises involves a pack of playing cards and turning them over so they are face down. Choose one card and hold your hand over it, see if you can feel which colour it is – red or black? Keep going with this for up to six cards or more if you feel like it – you are never going to get the whole pack right, but it's quite a fun way of practising. I found the whole family wanting to join me on this exercise. They wanted to know what Mum was doing by holding her hand above a row of playing cards. Naturally they all thought I was mad, but then wanted to have a go themselves. Much to my indignation, I found my youngest son to be exceptionally good at it.

You can try to predict pretty much anything when you are practising your psychic ability, from guessing the exact time of day, to what happens next in a book or film. We do this most days without really thinking about it. So the next time you do it, just be more consciously aware that you are doing it and make a note if you are becoming more accurate.

<u>Guidance Tips</u>

The one big piece of advice with this exercise is to practise it as much as you feel comfortable with and do not try to receive big bits of information. I remember watching a series on TV once where the main character kept getting told that 'God was in the detail.' He was so busy looking for the bigger picture, that he was missing the little details that proved to be significant. This works in a similar way, so try to notice the smaller details around you. You will be surprised at how much you think you know, but actually don't!

For example, without looking at it, think about your watch and picture it in your mind. Does it have numbers, dots, stones, Roman Numerals or something else? Not sure? Then have a look now.

As you've just looked at your watch, where were the hands? What time was it?

You've only just looked at it, so it should be quite obvious what the time was, but maybe you didn't take in that information. If you managed both of these easily, then great, there's always one clever one!

Okay, picture your friend's front door. Does it have glass, or is it filled in and where is the letter box? If you managed this easily then that's great. By noticing the smaller details, the messages you get which are subtle will be much easier to identify. Sometimes it's the details that seem most insignificant which turn out to be the most important.

Chapter 2: Spirits, Spirits Everywhere and Not a Drop to Drink

I appreciate many of you are probably very wary about opening the spiritual flood gates and accidentally letting the spirits of 95th Regiment or Headless Harry into your home. Believe me, it's rarely that exciting! I thought it would be helpful therefore, if I could explain to you where spirits go, what they are, what they are not and what ghosts are. Once this was explained to me, it confirmed what I already believed and everything fitted into place. It also took away the fear factor. This can be a source of contention with some religions, so please do not start reaching for the kindling and firewood. At least get to Chapter 5 before totally condemning me. I'll try to keep this as basic as I can without getting too deep.

When we die our essence, or energy (soul), moves on to another plane, of which there are several in fact. We will be collected by someone who loves us; usually someone that we know. It often comes as a bit of a surprise for some people to discover they are in an afterlife, having departed their physical body, especially if they didn't believe there was an existence possible after death. Once in the afterlife they tend to be more 'alive' than they ever were before here on Earth. Now, depending on the life they led on Earth, it will determine what plane they will end up existing in once in the afterlife. If they led a very spiritual and harmonious life, then they will be on one level, and if they led a cruel life, which has been full of immoral acts, then they will end up on another level. So people who have had their lives taken through murder or acts of violence, or who have been treated very cruelly by a person, will not see that person in spirit, unless they want to forgive that person. Before you hit the panic button, hitting your classmate when you were 7yrs old does not count as an evil act, neither does kissing someone other than your husband or wife at the Christmas party! I am referring to appalling acts of violence, or the sorts or crime that would have you looking at bars for a very long time.

Most of us will end up in a mid-level plane and exist in a beautiful, peaceful and harmonious place. This will look however we want it to look. I would like my heaven to be beautiful gardens, meadows, lakes, mountains and a large cottage overlooking the sea. Somewhere where I can bake an abundance of cakes and eat them without getting fat! You may prefer to have a floating gin palace that sails around beautiful islands in calm seas, beneath warm sunshine. In fact I may pop in for a G&T or two. Well, it would be rude not to. We will still have our loved ones around us, but we may see our 'heaven' differently to theirs. We will also look how we felt at our best when alive. For me I would like to be 32 years old again; a yummy mummy who is very short and petite, or as my eldest son would say, 'well fit'! In fact much skinnier than the short dumpy version I have since replaced the 'fit' one with.

There is no pain, no jealousy or illness. Spirits who were disabled, or who were ill whilst alive will no longer have those disabilities or illnesses when they have passed on. Mediums, however, will be able to see the spirit as they were when they were last alive. This is so that a living person is able to recognise the spirit when described. If your Grandma was in a wheelchair when she was last alive, there is no use in a medium describing a bouncy 25yr old blonde lady with fabulous legs. You will have no idea who they are talking about. She may be like that now in spirit, but if communicating through a medium, she will give impressions of how you would most recognise her. She will probably tell you that she has fabulous legs and all her own teeth again, and that she and Grandpa have been tripping the light fantastic, but she will show herself as she looked just before she died. The afterlife is certainly not to be feared; if anything it should be considered as something to look forward to. Think of it as the holiday or life you have always dreamt of, sharing it with the people who love you the most who have also passed over.

Children and babies will, too, be collected by someone who loves them, even those who were miscarried or terminated. Just as life is created and energy is made, that created energy will pass over into the find that they connect to a spirit that would have been the age of the child if still living. This is often confusing for the recipient of the message, because they think that the child will still remain at the age they were when they passed over. The recipient often dismisses the spirit and will tell the medium that they are wrong, that they do not know anyone of 8 years old for example, because their child died as a baby. Therefore it's often worth checking what age the child would be if alive, because if this happens to you and you feel the spirit of an older person then it's probably relevant.

I did a reading recently for a lady where I felt a spirit of around 30 years of age connected to her. She said she could not place the spirit, so I connected again and asked the spirit a few questions. The spirit gave me the word 'sister', so I asked her if she had a sister in spirit to which she replied yes she did, but she had died as a teenager. When I asked if her sister would be around 30 now, she said that yes she would be around that age and so I continued with the connection. When you connect to the spirit world yourself, it is worth remembering that a child will continue to grow up in spirit, and will often feel like the age they would have reached if alive. You will feel like you are in the presence of a person that is more mature. When they reach an age where they feel happy, they will not look older, but continue to exist in the spirit world. So for example, a baby who dies at a young age may continue to age in the spirit world and be content to look about 25 Earth years. They will continue to exist, but not look any older. Why would they? If you could stay looking 25, but actually be 65 years old, wouldn't you prefer to look younger? This may be a little complicated, so hopefully you are not reading this with a blank face!

One thing that always makes me smile is that some people think that just because a person has died, they will automatically become this wonderfully serene and virtuous person. If a person was tight-fisted, aggressive and generally unpleasant whilst alive, then it's quite likely that they will come across in spirit the same way. Remember it's their energy that has passed on, it's their essence, the bit that makes them who they are and this will be the same in death. They may be remorseful or apologise for their actions, which is absolutely great, but then again they may not. I have seen several readings where a spirit has come through and been more than a little frosty. For example, an ex-mother-in-law, who was still quite grumpy about the fact that her ex-daughter-in-law had walked out of the marriage to her son, had no problem in remaining indignant with her in spirit. Mediums cannot control the messages they get; it would be great if they were all messages of lottery wins and love, but they are not. Messages are usually for guidance, comfort, to say sorry or to let us living folk know that our loved ones are okay.

You will not be judged in the spirit world, whatever you have done, and you will only see those spirits you want to see. We are all here on Earth to learn, so will judge ourselves. If we have committed a hideous crime and hurt many people, then we will be on another plane to those we have hurt. Only when we have been forgiven by those we have hurt, can we move on to a higher plane. So people who have committed terrible atrocities, for example Adolf Hitler, will be a very, very long time on a lower level plane until forgiven by every single person he hurt and murdered, if he is ever forgiven.

Ghosts, on the other hand, are a memory of an event that has been marked in time. No amount of cleansing, exorcising or pounding of spiritual drums is going to move the ghost on, because technically there is nothing there other than a memory. Some events are so horrific or terrible that the imprint has been left there, which is why so many castles are haunted. Lots of people tended to die quite horribly. The negative energy that was felt at that time has been left there and can be felt or seen in later years. It's a little like a tape recording being played over and over again. This is why some ghosts are seen at the same time of day in the same locations.

Some spirits, however, are Earth bound and these are different to ghosts. Some do n that their loved ones have accepted the death, or until the loved one has passed on as well. Some spirits are too afraid to pass over; it may be that they believe so strongly that there is no such thing as an afterlife, that they fear going over. Others may have led a very materialistic life and do not want to leave their possessions behind. There can be numerous reasons for spirits wanting to stay and these spirits mediums *can* talk to. They can persuade them that the afterlife is nothing to fear, and that it's okay to move on.

It can be quite distressing for a number of people who can feel the presence of a spirit, particularly when it's in their home and if they do not want to communicate with the spirit. This is quite often not as dramatic as it first seems to be, with many people complaining of hauntings and poltergeist activity, when it is in fact much simpler. It's quite usual to inform family members and friends when you sense a presence of a spirit, if it's something that you fear. They then also become afraid and before you know it, mass hysteria has broken out. Jody has been called in to several houses to help move a spirit on, or to communicate with the spirit to find out why they are there. She was once called in to a lady who had experienced unusual happenings upstairs in her home, which for a number of years had been fittingly 'normal'. The lady had spoken to her family about the activity and in no time at all the whole family were terrified out of their wits. When Jody went upstairs in the lady's house, she ended up speaking to the woman's Grandfather. He informed her that the lady concerned had experienced three miscarriages, one of which was recent; he wanted to comfort her and be around her. When Jody passed this message on, the lady's first reaction was one of shock. The fact that Jody knew she had miscarried was something she had not expected and her second reaction was one of relief. As soon as the woman acknowledged her Grandfather and let him console her, in a manner of speaking, all activity calmed down.

Just because our loved ones pass on, it does not mean they do not want to comfort us. They can feel when we are upset or distressed and probably feel upset, too. Many people say that they have felt the presence of a loved one when they are feeling very sad or upset. To me this is quite logical, as I know for certain that I would want to comfort my loved ones if I had died. I would want them to know that I was there with them, even if I could not say anything. My mother has also said that she would come back and say hi. This is quite ironic really as we already call her the exorcist – she happily rids my house of all spirits, gin being a firm favourite!

When you tap into the spirit world and messages come through to you, they may be too fast, too slow, or need fine tuning, but this is all quite normal. You will *not* start levitating above your bed, your head will *not* rotate 360°, and you will *not* have Roman armies marching through your bedroom. If this were the case, then I am quite sure all of the news channels would have picked up something by now and it would definitely be common knowledge throughout the world. If you should get a message that you are not sure about, or you get a spirit who you are not keen on, then tell them to go away. I have no qualms about telling a spirit to 'go away', or letting them know that I am not interested. I'm quite happy to say that I am closed for business, but will be open again tomorrow if they want to drop in. I then imagine my spiritual energy flowing out of me in waves and then surrounding myself in white light; this seems to work well. If it's during daylight hours, then I will go outside. For me there is no better way of grounding myself, or switching off, than by going outside and joining in the normality of life. Going outside and being next to tarmac, street lights, plants and trees, is a good way to bring you back to reality.

Still with me? Hopefully your brain isn't too boggled at the moment. I appreciate that this may be different to how you imagined, but I think it really helps to know what you are dealing with. There are so many accounts of poltergeists and other such stories that it can be really scary to even contemplate communicating with those who have passed on and it shouldn't be. If you go into this with some knowledge of what you are doing, it makes practising easier and eliminates some of the fear. All you are doing is passing messages from one person to another, one just happens to not be alive. You are the 'go between' passing those messages, hence the term 'medium'. You are the middle bit. Think of it as getting a text message through for someone else and then telling that person the message. It really can be as simple as that and not something terrifying at all.

Exercise 2 – Psychometry

Whenever we handle an object we imprint that object with information about us, a bit like a recording. So items that we always have with us or that we are in constant contact with such as jewellery, keys, wallets and clothing, contain information about us that a medium or psychic can sense. You will often see this method used by those mediums and psychics that work with the police in tracing missing persons. It is also used when establishing what has happened to those people who have been victims of crime, such as murder. By having an object, the psychic can 'play back' the events and gather information about the owner of the object.

Buildings give off a similar energy and take on the energy of the people and events that have been inside. When I used to be a district nurse, I had to go into people's homes to visit them and would sense a whole range of emotions associated with the building. For anyone who has been house hunting you will know exactly what I am talking about when I say that some houses have a bad vibe about them. Some houses simply don't feel like a happy home, whereas others feel homely and welcoming. When you go through the door and you feel comfortable, quite often you will visualise the house with your furniture and imagine what Christmas would be like there. You picture a Christmas tree with lights and presents and it feels like a happy home. It's no coincidence that certain buildings feel welcoming, whilst others feel intimidating or downright miserable, because you are picking up on the emotions and energies felt by the people who have been in these places. Anyone who has been to visit a castle will probably find that some of the rooms felt quite pleasant and comfortable yet others felt frightening or depressing. That is because these were the emotions that were predominantly felt within those rooms.

Try this for yourself by 'feeling' the energy of a building – what are you picking up? It may be that it's something in between comfortable and 'get me out of here', so don't worry if you pick up a range of emotions as most will have a combination.

Alternatively, try psychometry for yourself by asking a family member or friend for an object that belongs to someone they know, but you do not. If possible try to ask for an object such as a watch, a ring, a set of keys, or something similar that they would keep with them or wear regularly. If you cannot get an object from someone you do not know it's much harder to tell if the information you are receiving is information you know already or facts that you are sensing. Try to find somewhere quiet where you can concentrate on the object. Place the object in your hand and feel the object. Some people prefer to use their less dominant hand as they find the messages are clearer. Use whichever hand you prefer by trying both. If thoughts or images come to mind then just make a note of them. If you prefer to, write down all of the images and emotions you sense so that you can review them later. Do not try to understand the images if at first they don't make much sense to you. You may get strong emotions attached to the object or just the odd image that pops into your head; again this is quite normal. You are not going to see a whole range of pictures, especially in the beginning, so do not be too frustrated if you do not sense much. The more you try this exercise, the easier you will find it and the more accurate you will become. Your mind will start to become used to 'seeing' the information.

If you find you simply sense nothing, or very little about the object you are holding, try to work with a photograph of someone who is no longer alive. Can you associate a significant month? The months we are given are usually a birthday, an anniversary of theirs, or a family member's. Sometimes it can be the month in which they died. Also try to find out how they died; if you have any physical sensations related to this, then make a note of them. Are you sensing any information about their life at all? Did they have children? What was their occupation? How do they make you feel, is it a good feeling or are you a little wary of them?

Guidance Tips

I struggled with this exercise when I first tried it in our group, and much to my absolute dismay, I received very little information from the ring I was holding. The lady next to me, however, was like a pressure cooker bubbling over and about to pop. If this happens to you do not worry as believe me, I know it can be frustrating. I find I can read a building incredibly easily, yet give me a bunch of keys and I may be able to get a male or female associated with them and sometimes the odd factual snippet. Psychometry does get easier with time and practice, like any new skill really. I know I keep stating this but do not rush it! If it feels right stick with it, and if it doesn't, then it may not be for you.

I tried one exercise where you asked someone you trusted to bring a stone or pebble for you to 'read'. You weren't supposed to sense a person, it wasn't quite that difficult, but you had to feel where the stone had come from. Was it near water? Was it from an area with trees or plants, that kind of thing? I sat with this stone firmly in my hand for minutes asking spirit if it came from a wooded area, or place of planting. All I could 'see' was dog poo; no matter what I did my mind kept coming up with images of dogs. So after half an hour of literally seeing 'poo' and the odd plant, I gave up and decided that maybe rocks and pebbles just were not for me. It did provide my husband with much merriment however, so at least one of us got something out of it!

I did find that I could work extremely well with photographs though. In my development circle one week we all brought in photos of a loved one who had passed over and swapped them with each other. As soon as I looked at the photograph, something clicked into place for me. I had a photograph of two people, who were clearly a couple, and I could tell quite quickly which of the two had passed on. I could sense the nature and character of the man straight away; it was a little like reading a book for me. I work mainly with photographs now when I do e-mail readings and find this method very successful. The more I work with photographs, the easier I find them. To me they just give so much information. I know that this method is not for everyone, some mediums absolutely hate working with photographs, so it really is a case of trial and error.

Try both of these methods and see what works for you. Only a few of us in the group, when we practised this exercise, had an affinity with photographs. Others preferred to work with personal items. Some didn't like either method, which may well be the case for you. Try out both techniques and see if you find you have a preference. Just remember that information can take a little while to filter through, so patience is required. If you start to get something, keep with it. It took me months and months of practising before I found the information flowing easily.

Chapter 3: Meditation – Love it or Hate it

Meditation is referred to in pretty much every one of the spiritual books I have ever read. Achieving a state of total calm will permit the spiritual airways to open and allow you to tune in to the spirit frequency. It's just like tuning a radio to begin with and the signal may be weak and distorted. With practice and some tweaking of your spiritual aerial, however, you will start to pick up the signals clearly. I will certainly be chastised by hardcore spiritualists for saying this, but for me and all in our development circle, we found that it was not essential to meditate first, as over time we still found we could still receive information. You **do** have to reach a relaxed state to be able to tune into the spirit frequency and meditation certainly makes communicating with spirit easier, so it's definitely recommended in the early stages. Put a different way, when I used to teach I would insist that students turn their mobile phones off. They could not concentrate on what was being taught or engage themselves fully if they were texting their friends. Now from a spirit's point of view, they cannot communicate as effectively with you if you are not concentrating or focusing on what they are saying. It's like you are focusing on two different tasks at once, so the messages can become confused. By meditating first you are clearing your mind and opening up the gateway between our world and theirs. Communication with spirit is not like having a chat over a coffee, unfortunately. It takes a lot of effort and you do need to focus. It has taken me three years to start getting clear messages, so prepare yourself for a slow process.

Some people struggle with meditation and can find it quite off putting that they cannot switch off. If this is the case with you, then refer to the Pranic breathing exercise at the end of this chapter as this will be useful. You also only need to work at this for 5 minutes or so in the first stages. If you try meditating for any longer, you will probably find your mind drifting off and the trivialities of the day will start to infiltrate your thoughts.

Most people like to meditate before doing a reading as their messages are much clearer afterwards. Meditation is not quite as hard as you think it might be, so I have included a really simple exercise below. It's not about emptying the mind totally and thinking about absolutely nothing; instead it's about finding a way of relaxing and calming your mind, so that you are open to receiving information. There are many, many books on meditation, which may differ slightly to what is written here. However this is the one that I have found by far the easiest and most effective to learn.

Exercise 3 - Meditation Made Easy

Start by finding somewhere clean and quiet where you will not be disturbed for 5-10 minutes, particularly if you are new to this. Sounds of the television or children playing can easily distract you and a cluttered room can result in cluttered thoughts. It's not essential to tidy the room within an inch of its life, or rid the area of all noise. The odd bit of traffic noise and clutter is not going to matter that much. If you can find somewhere totally clean and quiet then it's a bonus, but it is certainly not essential and something I have never managed!

If you have some relaxing music you can play softly in the background, this may help to calm and relax you. Meditation music is widely available and for me it definitely helps. Music with words will be too distracting and you will soon be singing along or thinking of the words, so instrumental works best. Classical music is also fine as long as it's not too sombre or has rousing crescendos, as this can affect your mood and concentration. Ideally what you are looking for is something uplifting and calming. I find music used for Reiki healing or meditating is perfect.

I have kept this meditation very simple so that you can imagine it easily without having to refer back to what is written. Read through it first then find somewhere quiet to practise it. Take your time in completing each part if you feel content to do so. You can extend this meditation should you choose to, as long as you feel you can concentrate on the images.

Once you have your quiet place and you have your music on, sit comfortably in an upright position within your room. You do not have to sit on the floor with your legs crossed. You can sit in a chair with your legs uncrossed and with a straight back. The energy needs to be able to flow through you, which is why sitting upright is better. Start by concentrating on your breathing. Breathe in through your nose deeply and exhale fully. This can be back through the nose or through the mouth, then close your eyes. If you prefer to have your eyes partially open, that is absolutely fine and is often recommended; work with whatever you prefer. Lay your hands on your lap in an open position and concentrate on your breathing.

Meditation

Imagine you are in a beautiful meadow on a warm, sunny day. The sky is blue and you can hear birds chirping all around you. There are beautiful wild flowers in the meadow and you can feel the warmth of the sun on your back and head. You can see several trees in the meadow, which are green and bursting with life. There is a small trickling stream nearby. It has crystal clear water flowing through it. You feel totally relaxed and calm here and notice a deep, fluffy blanket which you decide to sit down on. You feel safe and warm, completely content where you are. Look up at the blue sky and breathe in deeply for a moment. You notice a small, fluffy cloud drift overhead and see that it's a different colour than usual. It's a colour that feels energising and uplifting. Watch the cloud drift over and rest just above you. A very fine warm mist of the same colour drifts down over you and gently soaks into your body. It fills you with a warm glow and energy that flows through your body. You feel absolutely peaceful, energised and calm. Relax for a moment as the energy gently flows through you. Stay here quietly for a minute if you feel content to do so. Watch as the cloud slowly rises up into the sky and slowly drifts away again. The sun is still shining warm and bright, your breathing is slow and full. You can hear the birds around you and the stream trickling gently nearby. You can feel the energy flowing through you, which leaves you feeling totally relaxed and glowing within. Slowly concentrating on your breathing, begin to open your eyes. Gradually become aware of the room you are in and note how you feel totally refreshed.

After you have relaxed your mind you can begin to focus on any messages you begin to receive from the spirit world. If you are reading for someone, carry out this exercise first and hopefully you will get a better connection.

In the beginning you may find that your mind is busy with lots of other thoughts popping in to it, which is quite normal! In time you will find this exercise easier and your mind will feel more open to the images you are putting in it. When I first started this I would find I could concentrate for about a minute and then my mind would drift off. I would start thinking about what I needed to add to my shopping list, or I'd remember that I needed to chase up an invoice that had not been paid by a client. My mind would drift off to lots of general work or family tasks that needed completing. After a month or so of feeling frustrated with my inability to focus, I decided to take a pad and paper with me and write down the thoughts that popped into my head. By doing so I could concentrate more easily and now I don't need the pad and pen at all. Other people I know imagine a blackboard and write down the task or note to themselves mentally and then move on.

Whenever you feel your mind drift, concentrate on your breathing again; breathing in deeply and exhaling fully. Keep concentrating on your breathing until the image you last had of yourself in the meadow comes back. When you feel ready, you can move on to the next step. If you get stuck on a particular part of this scene and find it difficult to move on, then change it so that you can visualise it easily and become unstuck. It's not so much about following the scene exactly, but more about opening your mind and achieving a sense of total calm and well-being. Try not to get caught up in following the exercise to the letter. If by changing the scene to suit you, the results you achieve are the same, change the scene.

The one detail I struggled with was picturing a cloud of a different colour. I am not sure why exactly, but my mind was not having any of it and I would get 'stuck' on this image. By changing the cloud colour to a small fluffy white one with coloured mist coming down, I could follow the exercise and I have used this ever since. You may find that you cannot picture a stream clearly. If this is the case then take it out. You may find yourself being able to hear the stream, but not see it, and that, too, is absolutely fine. You may prefer to be in a meadow that is next to the sea, so if this is the case, then have it next to the sea. Use whatever works for you by adding details or removing them. It does take practice, but it will get easier, just like learning any new skill. Think of it as a new language; you would not be fluent after a month or so, it would take time and effort before becoming easier.

Once you have found that you can perform this exercise without difficulty, try to see more detail where possible. Look at the flowers or the trees, what do they look like? What colour are they? Try to imagine what the flowers smell like, or practise holding one. Picture its leaves and stem, and look at it in detail. The more you practise getting the details of a scene, the more you will be able to 'read' the messages you receive.

If you find that you simply cannot meditate, that for whatever reason you cannot maintain a focus, do not worry. Try instead to concentrate on your breathing. If you are asking yourself 'Why do I need to concentrate on my breathing? Surely I'd know if I wasn't breathing!' it's because most of us tend to breathe in quite shallow, rapid breaths, rather than deep and sustained breaths.

Here are some breathing exercises to try if you cannot meditate:

1. Stay sat in an upright position so that the energy can flow through you, from your bottom straight up through to the top of your head.

Have your palms open on your lap or on your tummy, whichever feels more comfortable. If you prefer to lay down with your knees bent, then this is also fine. The main point is to keep your torso straight.

2. Breathe in deeply through your nose and suck in your stomach so that your ribcage rises. The air should feel like it's coming from the bottom of your abdomen.

3. Hold it briefly, and then breathe out slowly through your nose, fully, so that your abdomen pushes out (or bulges in my case!).

4. Keep repeating this for a few minutes. This should help you achieve a spiritual connection before beginning clairvoyance.

This is a simple form of Pranic breathing which allows you to focus on making a good connection with the spirit world. It's perfect if you find that meditation is not for you, as you should still be able to connect to spirit quite successfully.

Chapter 4: Seeing Red?

When I first heard Jody talk about auras, I must admit I did think that she had lost the plot and I had come to the advanced class. When she described a method for the group to start getting *used to the idea* of auras by reading people as colours, it actually made sense and can help with your development. Trust me on this one, keep reading and hopefully you will see what I mean.

An aura refers to the radiance or energy field that comes from the surface of any living person or being and is seen as an outline of different colours. The human body does give off radiations, including electromagnetic signals, which have been scientifically proven, so there is some fact behind the principle. To put this simply, it's similar to looking at the boy on television who has eaten a certain instant porridge for breakfast. It's the young lad with a lovely orange glow around him. The main difference is that auras are made up of a range of colours, some of which are more dominant than others. When reading an aura, the colour pattern is said to be dependent on an individual's well-being. This includes their chemical, emotional, physical, and spiritual state.

To learn to see auras properly, you are meant to sit a person in front of a white background that is gently lit and stare at that forehead for approximately 30-60 seconds. You are then meant to see a range of colours around them in your peripheral vision as you stare at their forehead. Personally when I read about this, I thought that there was no way I was going to find a white wall and ask someone sit down in front of it, whilst I stared at their forehead. I am not sure who would have felt more of a twit. I am not saying that I doubt people who claim they see energies or auras. It's just that I couldn't see myself doing it. It felt a little too advanced for me and I did not feel at all ready. It is something I would considered as a separate class that you attend over time, should this be of interest to you. You do not need to be able to read auras in order to be a good clairvoyant and this is not a method for reading auras.

What Jody suggested though, was to *associate* a colour with a person, rather than trying to see the colour. Colours do affect how we feel and all of us have colours that we absolutely love and those that we hate. They are different for all of us and you will probably find that the clothes you are drawn to are predominantly one colour. This is because that particular colour seems to suit you and you feel good in that colour. The main factor here is that you associate an emotion or feeling with the colour that is relevant to you. Do not be put off by associating an emotion to a colour that is different from how you imagined it to make you feel. For example, some people feel that black is very negative, or that red indicates an angry aggressive colour, green is healthy and so on. It can mean the complete opposite when you apply an association to it.

Now you may be thinking, 'Why would I want to associate a colour with someone?' The rationale behind it is that when you communicate with spirits, they may show you images, symbols, or colours that will trigger a reaction. The other reason is that when you do a reading for someone, you may feel a particular colour with them which would link to an emotion or state of health. For example, if I picture a grey colour with a person, I know they are unwell or have been ill recently. I do not see it, but I associate it and feel it. If I picture black with a person, I associate it with grief, it's the colour I felt when I was grieving. It's almost a way of checking someone's emotional state before you have even spoken to them. It gives you an idea of what that person is feeling and helps when you are reading for someone.

When I started associating colours with people in our development group, we would all meditate for 5 minutes, using the meditation in chapter 3, and then choose someone who we felt drawn to. Each time we did this, several of us would pick out the same person. We would go around in turn and say who out of the group we had picked, and describe the colour and emotion we felt around the person. For those of us who quite often picked the same person, we would find that the emotions associated were very similar, but the colours were different.

One lady in our group was picked out by five of us and was mainly associated with either pink or yellow. The colours, although different, had almost the same meanings for us. She was feeling very happy, content and was a bright and bubbly young lady. It was a very positive feeling we were all getting from her despite many of us choosing different colours. This is why it's essential that *you choose* the colour that fits the emotion, rather than being told what you should be feeling when associating a colour to emotions.

For me, dark green is a strong and healthy colour, whereas others hate it and sense an entirely different emotion, so it really depends on what the individual person feels.

Exercise 4 – Seeing in Colour

For this exercise, you need to pick out a person that you are drawn to. It does not have to be someone you know; it can be any person at all. Try to associate a colour with them. Do they look happy or excited and if so what colour would that be for you? If you see young children playing in the sunshine, what colour would you choose for them? Remember you are not seeing the colour, but feeling it. You may see someone queuing at a till and notice they are getting impatient; you can almost feel their negative thoughts coming your way, particularly if you are the person in front! What colour would you picture around that person?

The more you do this, the more you will associate feelings with colours and begin to feel the colour, or colours, around that person. This works well after meditating for 5 minutes first so you are more open to feeling a person's emotions. It can be a little difficult though if you decide to practise in a queue in a supermarket. The wines and spirits aisle is not the best place to begin a quick 5 minute meditation before practising your new skill!

A person's aura is usually made up of an array of colours, so start off with feeling just one colour. If you could pick one colour for that person, what would it be and what emotion or feeling do you identify with it? You may find you get one or two colours and that's fine. If you get a whole rainbow, try to pick out the most dominant colours that you get then associate a feeling or emotion with them. Remember this is not actually reading a person's aura, but instead you are beginning to work with colour, and relating emotions to that colour.

Guidance Tips

If, in the beginning, you do not get any colour with the person, then move on to someone you do connect with. If you are unsure of how that colour makes you feel, picture yourself in a room of that colour only. How do you feel in the room? Does it make you feel warm or calm, or does it make you feel claustrophobic, like you want to get out quickly?

Try to associate a colour with an emotion or general feeling. I found it really helpful to write down what emotions I felt with certain colours, and would practise associating the feeling with the colour. Now when I see people I know, I tend to picture colours around them. I have the most wonderful friend who for me is mostly dark green, pale blue and bright blue, lilac and silvery white. She is very fit and healthy, has a fantastic husband and family that she adores. She loves nature and is quite a spiritual person. She is also the most honest and sensitive person I have ever met, a very gentle lady. Someone else may picture completely different colours around her, but I am totally convinced they would see very similar qualities.

You will most likely find that you will only ever use a few predominant colours, but that the ones you use will be accurate each time. If I see a baby that is due, I will usually get the feeling of being pregnant with a little bump for a conception, or a big bump if the baby is due very shortly. I then picture a baby with a pink blanket or a blue blanket wrapped around them to determine a boy or a girl. If I see black, then I know a person is recently bereaved or grieving hard. If I see purple, then I know the person is very spiritual or sensitive to spirits themselves. It's just a matter of trying this yourself and paying attention to how you feel. Take note of the colours that spring to mind when you feel certain emotions. Don't try to read too much into it if at first an emotion does not come easily, because it's not essential for clairvoyance. It's useful as an aid and can help determine a person's state of mind when coming for a reading.

Chapter 5: Spirit Guides

Now if you have raced ahead to this section of the book, itching to find out how to connect with your spirit guide and find out more about who they are, then you are very much like how I started out. There are a heap of books and information about how to connect with your spirit guide and how to prepare for the journey that you will take with them. So I am going to give you the condensed version that cuts out a lot of the heavy tree huggy bit that goes with it. Before I do, I want to tell you about my first experience of meeting with my spirit guide, because it was **nothing** like I imagined and yours may end up being somewhat similar.

For months and months I tried to connect with my spirit guide after reading numerous books about meditating and practising for what seemed like hours on end. I would sit there every week, concentrating on my breathing with my Chakras lined up (we'll cover Chakras later), hoping for enlightenment. I would be thanking every angel, guardian angel, archangel and guide imaginable, for allowing me to try to make a connection to them. I would also try to surround myself in a white protective light whilst also blocking out any unwanted entities. I had, after all, seen the film 'The Exorcist', and was hoping to keep my head facing front on! Whatever it was I was doing, I felt I must be doing it wrong because not much was happening.

I avidly read one book in particular as it was purely about connecting with your guide and had sold thousands of copies. It near as damn it guaranteed that I would be chatting with grandma in no time at all. The book recommended daily meditation, which I tried my best to stick to. These would progress in length and difficulty until such time that I was ready for the big one; the one meditation exercise in which I would meet my spirit guide and this event was going to give me a huge sense of all-encompassing love and well-being. The book hyped me up so much, that I was practically bouncing with excitement that I would finally meet him or her. I carefully chose my moment. The room was candle lit, I had gentle music playing and I started meditating as I had been previously. I went into my 'magical cave' and waited patiently, just as the book suggested. I waited a bit more, but after not getting anything I figured that I had either got it wrong or that my spirit guide was detained somewhere. After a few more minutes, I had the feeling of a man with me who was quite young, around 30years old or so and felt that this was a good sign. The image unfortunately, was not clear at all, but I decided to continue with my meditation. My book advised me to ask all of those deep and meaningful questions I had been waiting for, once he or she had made an appearance. So I started a mental conversation in my head that went something like this:

Me: 'Am I imagining this or are you my actual guide?'

Him: 'What do you think, I guess I could be?'

Me: 'I thought it would be more, um, clear than this and more overwhelming, this doesn't feel right, I am talking to myself really aren't I?'

Him: 'Well you could be.'

Me: 'Okay then, what should I call you?'

Him: (silence)

Me: 'Any name you like.'

Him: 'Bob.'

Me: 'No that's not right, I've made that up. Let's me try again.'

(Interrupted by son briefly)

Me: 'Sorry I'm back, where were we? Names, okay, not Bob.'

Him: 'Walt, short for Walter.'

Me: 'Walter! Really? I was expecting something more mystical, no offence?'

Him: 'None taken and yes, Walter.'

Me: 'Okay Walter, I am meant to take note of what you're wearing here, but I'm not getting anything at all. I mean you're not naked, but I can't picture what you are wearing. Crikey, this is really hard. I don't think I'm doing this right.'

Walter: 'You need to be patient, Amy.'

Me: 'Hmmmm okay, could you give me a message or something I can take with me?'

Walter: (silence)

Me: 'Okay. Maybe next time then, thank you for visiting me.' (At this point I was thinking that I was really not very good at this exercise at all).

After this I wondered whether or not I had imagined the whole conversation, or if this was actually my guide. Looking back at that conversation, it's clear to me that I doubted the very fact that it was my guide because my own logical thoughts kept popping into my head. It was only over time that I found the same guide kept coming back and working with me. Eventually I trusted the fact that he was with me and we developed a good relationship. The key thing here is to accept the first pieces of information you are given. It's easy to doubt them, but you will have been given the information for a reason.

Now if your visit goes something like this, please do not rule it out or feel disappointed. I doubted every message I was getting and sometimes it was so hard to distinguish between what I was receiving and my imagination that I would drive myself nuts with frustration. Some of the answers I would get were so obvious that I thought that I was bound to think them up myself, others were total gibberish and I couldn't understand them. It was just too confusing. Over time I began to see Walter in an army uniform and he told me that he was involved in World War II. I never did get the gist of whether or not he died during the war or had a long happy life. To be honest I was never sure if he was a figment of my imagination or not, but either way I would talk to him and meet up with him in my mind. I would not go to my 'magical' cave, but instead I would picture us sitting together on a bench out near to Portland Bill. It's a place I love to visit, looking out to sea, over to where my Dad's ashes are scattered. I would chat to him about all sorts of bits and pieces involved with my spiritual development, (or lack of it), and he, in turn, would listen and often laugh at my frustrated ramblings.

I suppose that what I am getting at, is do not expect a huge fanfare if you are starting out. Your guides can often work so subtly, it's easy to dismiss a lot of it, or think that you are imagining it. If you do get some solid information, then that's fantastic. You are obviously more than ready to work with your guide, but if you do not, then just accept (begrudgingly) that it will take time. Once I had accepted Walter, I just kept working with him. I would talk through some of the messages I had received with Walter to see if he could enlighten me about many of them. He didn't always give me answers, or explain who it was speaking, or why they had contacted me to begin with. He was more of a friend that I could sound off to because my friends and family would more than likely think I had lost the plot if I spoke to them. Over time I learned to trust Walter and I loved talking to him; he was more of a great friend who was there for me whilst I was struggling away to make sense of it all. Your guides will do the same with you, and they will work with you at a level that you will be comfortable with. There's no point in taking an A level French class if you have not mastered basic conversational French. This is exactly the same principle. The difficulty here is that you think you are ready and want the information to come through loud and clear. They, on the other hand, know you are not ready and will only work with you at an advanced level, when *they* feel the time is right.

So who are these guides that work with us?

After much research and asking of questions, I feel that the theory below is the easiest way of explaining who spirit guides are and why they work with us. There will be numerous variations, but I feel this is the most accurate.

Guides are most often spirits who have previously lived on this plane, or Earth as we like to call it, on various occasions. They have probably had numerous experiences of life and will have acquired a lot of knowledge of what we Earthly folk go through. They have learned a wealth of information over time, which is why they are guides now and have a lot to share about spiritual development. They have decided that they will help someone to develop their clairvoyance and spirituality when picking a career in the spiritual job centre and they are hoping to find a willing pupil. They are there to help us develop and also to protect and nurture us – a bit like having a teacher at school. They will be there to make sure we develop at a suitable pace. They check that information is given to us in a manner that we can relate to, hoping that over time, we learn to trust and work with them. Just like school, it's a two way street – the more you put in, the more you get out, but it can take a little while before you graduate. You will find that your guide may share similar qualities as you; they may share the same sense of humour and they will be of a similar intellect, for example. There is no use in pairing up someone who hates anything educational with a guide who is a total academic and loves facts. The more like you they are, the more you will be able to relate to them. They may have had a totally different Earth- bound job when alive, but there will be a good reason why they have chosen you to work with. There will be a connection that is right for the two of you to work together. They will always be there when you need them, but they will not constantly be with you for 24hours a day, it's not necessary. They may also have other work they have to do, just like a teacher, which will keep them busy.

I always thought there would be some deep and meaningful reason why Walter chose me, but in fact it was as simple as mainly being there to listen to me and to share a laugh together. Although this was mainly at my expense! His main lesson for me was to learn patience as I wanted everything straight away. I had watched Allison DuBois in the TV show 'Medium' doing her bit and I wanted to do my bit, too!

Guides are not all going to be as you expect them to be. They are not all Native American Indians with long and profound names, such as Two Dancing Feathers or Great Fighting Bear. Do not be surprised if the first name you get is Fred or something really odd sounding such as Urph. Many books I read told me that the name was not really important. It was more to do with the fact that we know we are working with someone that is most crucial. This is actually true. Some people never get a name, but still work quite happily with their guides. You may decide like me, that you want to change their name and, again, this is fine too. Think of it this way; many children when they are little call their grandparents a different name to grandma or grandpa. This is usually because they cannot say the grandma or grandpa properly. They choose a name that they can say and then the name sticks. It does not change the relationship at all. My cousin's little girl calls her grandpa 'Bubby', because she could not manage' Grand-Dad' when she was little. She is actually much older now and at school, but the name has still stuck and never been changed. So don't worry if you decide that you do not take to a name or feel that you have it wrong. The main point is that you call them by whatever you feel is right. If you are comfortable with a name then keep with it; I guarantee they will not mind.

So how does your guide work? Personally, this is probably the easiest explanation and one theory that I find most people can identify with. Imagine you are trying to connect to the spirit world through a telephone, you are at one end and the spirit you are connecting with is at the other end. Your guide will be the telephone enabling the connection, linking the two of you together. Now, unlike a phone conversation with your best friend, you will not get all of your messages through in a long clear conversation. This is a bit of a pain, but unfortunately that's how it works. Instead of a long conversation, you will be getting snippets of information, some of which won't mean a thing to you and your guide will be able to help at times to try to decipher the message. It doesn't always work, although they will do their best. You also need to remember that there will be times when we will misinterpret a message. I never really understood why some messages would come through crystal clear and yet others would leave me, or the person I was reading for, totally baffled. Some messages will be confusing for the medium, but will make sense to the person being read to, so please don't worry about understanding the message. Some messages will make sense to the person later, but not at the time or possibly not at all. It's unfortunate but it is part of the process.

One reading I did for a lady, Niki, showed me an image of my necklace. This is something which is very dear to me, as it contains some of my Dad's ashes. So I gave Niki the message that she possibly had a piece of jewellery belonging to her father, who had passed on, which looked like it was possibly a necklace. I had a very baffled face looking back at me which threw me off course. I tried again and kept getting my necklace shown to me, which was infuriating because I could not understand what her Dad was trying to show me. Niki told me she had been given 3 items belonging to her father, but jewellery was not one of them. I tried to connect again, but just had the same image. I finally managed to piece together the message that she had something which had belonged to him, that she felt strongly connected to him through. It was something she had of his that she could feel his presence through, as I do with my necklace. I did get a brief image of a guitar, but as he was a guitarist I felt this to be too obvious and dismissed it. As soon as she said yes to me, that she did have something of his that she could almost feel his presence through, I understood why he had showed me my necklace. It was the one item she had that she felt most connected to him. He had been telling me at the start of the reading that she could feel his presence at times and then he showed me my necklace. I just couldn't piece it together. When Niki showed me his guitar, I wanted to slap myself as I had been shown one very briefly, but dismissed it. Small details are important, so even if they appear obvious it's probably because they are. The rest of the reading was incredibly clear, right down to some very personal details. It would have been easy to have given up if I had been put off my interpretation of that one message.

Now the reason why spirits cannot come through clearly, I believe, is that that it would be too easy for us if they did; that there is a limit to what we Earthly folk are allowed to know. If we all knew that there was a definite afterlife that could be proven without a doubt, a place which was absolutely wonderful where we were surrounded by our loved ones, we would have everybody wanting to be there rather than here. It would defeat the whole object of living. For example, think about when people play a computer game. They do not care if they take other 'lives' or lose their own 'life', because the character gets regenerated after death and can do this time and time again. Some people play very recklessly using death defying moves or show no concerns for other characters in the game. They are safe in the knowledge that they can come back and have another go without suffering any consequences.

Now imagine the same principles in this life. If we knew unequivocally that there is an afterlife, we would also become very reckless with our own lives and that of others. We'd find ourselves giving up at the first hurdle and carrying out some drastic measures when coming up against situations we didn't like. I watched a programme once in which a lady had lost her son to a traffic accident and never got over it. She was so depressed without her son that she didn't feel like she would ever be happy again. She then met an angel who thought he could help her to be happy by showing her that her son was safe in the afterlife. She was so joyously happy that he was in spirit that she threw herself off a bridge and committed suicide, just so she could be with him. In the programme it was the angel's lesson to learn that humans do not benefit by knowing for certain there is an afterlife. It struck such a chord with me because I had been saying the exact same thing myself. I know this may be a new concept for you and might not sit well with you, but put simply we cannot fully know the full picture for sure as life would become too easy. Spirits therefore work on a very subtle level and will give you images that you have to interpret. Information will not come through like you are having a conversation, believe me, I wish it would!

I truly believe we are here to learn, that our lives on Earth are just like going to school in which we have lessons to learn before we can move back home. I feel that 'life' is us being away from 'home' when we are here on Earth and that when we die we go back 'home', not the other way round. The other thing is that we will work with different guides for different tasks. You won't have a whole house full of guides, but you will most likely work with two or three mainly, without even knowing it. Your clairvoyant guide will be different to your music guide, if you are an exceptional musician for example. If you are the sort of person who is not very good at something, such as drawing, then you will most likely not find yourself working with an art guide. There will, however, be *something* that you are exceptionally good at. We all have one talent. It could be that people find you easy to talk to or that you are a good listener. It does not always have to be something academic or creative, such as writing poetry or painting. It could be something that you do not attribute much value to, but it will be something you know you are good at. Whatever it is, it seems to come naturally to you. Personally, I love to cook; I find I can turn my hand to anything in the kitchen and it works. I listen to that inner voice that tells me 'take that out of the oven NOW and it will be perfect' and it is. I know have a female guide working with me in the kitchen and she is fabulous, she has been with me a long time and I totally love her! She is unlike my clairvoyant guide, who is equally fabulous in a totally different way. So if you are the sort of person who's told by your family, 'if they can't smell burning then it's salad for dinner', then you are probably not working with a culinary guide when you cook. Your guide will be with you and work with you to make a particular part of your life flourish.

In a similar way to how we learn here at school, your clairvoyant guides will change just as teachers change. When you went to primary school, your teachers would pass on their knowledge to you in a way that you could understand and develop. Then you would move on to another higher class, in which you would have a different teacher who would pass on their knowledge to you. This is the same with guides. Your guide will be right for you and your development at that particular stage. Once you have mastered that stage, you will get a new 'teacher' who will help you move on and develop further.

When I started going to my spiritual development group, I bumbled along in the first week or two quite happily. I was doing quite well but I was so eager to learn it was almost tangible- I was fit to pop! I could not wait for each session and felt like a giant sponge, ready to absorb as much information as Jody could possibly give me. I practised constantly and I felt that I was progressing well. Jody encouraged us all to work with what we felt was right and to trust what information we were getting. She explained what was likely to be imagination and what was not. It just seemed to click for me, like someone turning on a light switch after years of fumbling with a box of matches. So when we did a meditation exercise in which we met our guides, my images were not clear. I kept trying to picture Walter, but the scene would not 'play' properly. It was not clear at all. This was not what I was expecting; I was expecting to see Walter really clearly and we'd sit and chat like we always had done. I left the class that night feeling quite confused and anxious that Walter had left me, as for the first time he hadn't turned up.

The next meditation exercise we undertook, in which we met our guides again, I saw someone new waiting for me this time. I was quite taken aback to see it was not Walter, but was someone different. I must admit I was a bit shocked and wondered if my imagination had gone mad again, but there was the chap who looked totally different to Walter. We started to talk and he gave me his name, which again I questioned as it didn't feel right (fussy woman), so I asked again and then he gave me the name of David. Since then I can feel him so clearly when he is working with me and my clairvoyant work has taken off! He is superb and I love working with him, even though I thought Walter was wonderful and irreplaceable. David's information is clear and the messages I receive from spirit are always accurate. Sometimes my interpretation needs adjusting, but it's always right. I get those little nuggets of information that identifies clearly who the spirit is for the person I am reading for. For me, that is the best feeling in the world. David is quite an academic chap with a lovely soft, deep voice and he gives me information in a way that I can work comfortably with. So do not be surprised if you end up with a guide that is different from what you expect and do not be shocked if your guide changes. You would not have the same teacher in university as you would in primary school. There is only so much one person can teach you and it's exactly the same for your spirit guides. Once you have learnt all you can with one guide you will work with a new one and the more you embrace your learning, the more you will get out of it. Just think of it as going to spiritual school and you will be on the right track. Just don't forget to do your homework and drop in and talk to your teachers.

Exercise 5 – Meet Your Guide

This is going to be a meditation exercise, so you will need to be somewhere quiet again, where you will not be interrupted (if possible) for 10 minutes or so. I have simplified this meditation also, so you can follow it easily without referring back to what is written. Read through it first, then try and practise when you are ready.

Once you have found somewhere quiet, put relaxing meditation music on if it helps and sit comfortably upright, or lay down straight if you prefer. You do not have to sit on the floor with your legs crossed. You can sit in a chair with your legs uncrossed, with a straight back. The energy needs to be able to flow through you. Start by concentrating on your breathing. Breathe in through your nose deeply and exhale fully. This can be back through the nose or through the mouth, then close your eyes. If you prefer to have your eyes partially open that is absolutely fine and is often recommended; work with whatever you prefer. Lay your hands on your lap in an open position and concentrate on your breathing. Picture a white light shining out from the top of your head.

Imagine yourself walking along a beach on a warm day. You can feel the sand underneath your bare feet and around your toes. You are dressed in loose, comfortable clothing and feel totally relaxed. The sea is calm and clear. You can hear the water gently lapping back and forth over the sand, as you walk along the beach with the sun shining above you. Breathe in deeply. You can smell the sea air and you feel absolutely calm and happy. This is a beautiful place and somewhere that you feel very comfortable. There are large rocks dotted along the beach and you notice how they look.

As you continue along the beach, you see a small opening in a cliff to your left and you walk over to look at the opening and see where it leads. As you walk into the cave you see a bright white light further along and decide to go over to it. You pass through the white light and into another part of the cave with sand all along the floor. This cave is round and lit with lots of candles. It looks beautiful inside and welcoming; you are not afraid to go in. You go further into the cave and see a small seat. This seat has been carved out of the rock. It is totally smooth and comfortable, so you sit down on it. You begin to sense that someone has come into the cave with you. This person is someone very kind and helpful, someone that you would like to talk to, so ask them to come and sit next to you. Try to picture this person who has sat down next to you. Are they male or female, young or old, tall or short? How are they dressed? How do they make you feel? This will be your spirit guide.

If the image is not clear, do not worry as this will develop in time. Ask them for a name for you to call them by. This will come through like a thought in your head, not like a loud voice in your ear. Ask them if they have a message, or an object for you. Picture them handing you a piece of paper with something written or drawn on it and take note of what it says. If you are happy here and comfortable talking to your guide, then you can ask them other questions until you are ready to leave.

It's now time to leave the cave, so thank your guide for visiting you. Slowly stand up and leave the cave. Walk back through the light and out of the cave along the beach, feeling the sand underneath your feet and listening to the sound of the sea. The sun is warm on your face. Continue along the beach until you are ready to come back into your own space. Begin to feel yourself coming back to the room that you are in. When you are ready, open your eyes and find yourself back in your room. You feel very relaxed and calm.

Guidance Tips

When you start communicating with your guide, try to trust the information you are getting, even if it's different from what you expected. You *will* doubt some of the information you receive, and to be fair some of it may be your active imagination having a bit of a laugh at your expense. Try not to dismiss it, however, even if it's a little unusual. For example, if you received a message on the piece of paper, such as a symbol of a bus or a word such as 'cake', it may be exactly the word your guide wanted to say to you, rather than the long profound message you expected to receive. Think of it this way; when spirit communicates with you, it often comes through in images or words. So 'bus' for example, could be travelling and 'cake' could mean a celebration of some sort. If I saw those images then that is probably the meaning I would associate with them. Try to connect a meaning with any words or images that you are unsure of and it may make more sense. You may have had a lovely message from your guide explaining how pleased they are to work with you, or something similar. This is fantastic. It may be that you get nothing at all, but don't be put off. The more you visit your guide, the clearer the message will be.

Now if you did get a really odd message, such as 'Think like the llama and go to the one armed tree to dance in the moonlight with an orangutan named George ', I would question your message. This is more than likely to be your imagination playing a fantastic trick on you. It could be genuine, but more often than not your guide will give you subtle messages that mean something to you, otherwise what would be the point? I have never come across a message given like this, thankfully. Your guide is not going to give you a message that means absolutely nothing to you when you are asking them about your own development. You may have to work at the message a little, but it should not be so obscure or 'out there' that you feel you are questioning every single aspect of it.

The other thing you should start to look for is a sensation you can feel, when your guide is with you. You can ask them to give you a feeling you will recognise them by. This can be when you are in your cave if you wish, but I can guarantee that in time you will know exactly when they are with you. This will be subtle- and I do mean subtle! There will not be a big tap on the shoulder, or a loud voice saying 'I am here', I wish it were that simple. Instead, look out for a subtle sensation, such as a gentle stroke on the arm or face, a little like a small stroke from a feather or a tingling sensation. I feel a tingling sensation at the front of my head on the left hand side and when I call upon my guide, I experience that sensation almost instantly now. It took nearly two and a half years for me to get it that clear, so do not be surprised if you don't manage it straight away. When I worked with Walter, it was immensely subtle. Sometimes I could not always be sure he was even with me, but I trusted that he was. Now I am working with David, I have such a good connection with him. I trust him and sense him clearly, but it did take time. I needed to go through my newbie stage with Walter in order to get where I am now. By going through the learning process, I have learnt the difference between what is a spiritual connection and what my logical mind is trying to cut in.

If you find you cannot meditate and don't receive any information, then instead try to relax yourself by going somewhere quiet where you can take slow, deep breaths. Ask for your guide to make themselves known to you and see what happens. It may be that you only feel a sensation and not visualise anything. This is absolutely fine. As long as you begin to feel something, eventually, with time, this will begin to develop into a clearer feeling. It can take years to develop a relationship with your guide where you are totally confident and trust their method of communication with you. You will question a lot of information when you start out, in order to work out what's valid and reliable, so the next time you get that information you don't even question it.

I know it's difficult when you are starting out, but I have tried to keep it as simple as I can. I had so many questions when I began to work with my guide, so I am trying to cover as many I can that may help you. Hopefully you are not sitting there with a totally baffled look! I thought my brain was going to melt when I started delving deeper. So if yours is feeling similar, give yourself some time out and leave this for a while. Eat a pile of chocolate and remind yourself that you're only learning; you will start to feel better soon.

"Take the first step in faith.
You don't have to see the whole staircase.
Just take the first step."

Dr. Martin Luther King, Jr.

Chapter 6: Play Your Cards Right

There are many different ways of gathering information from the spirit world, some were mentioned earlier such as psychometry, or other methods such as Tarot cards. You will find once you have a connection you can 'read' pretty much anything from a handpicked flower to a roaring fire in order to communicate with spirit. It may sound strange, but trust me on this one. It has more to do with the connection than the method. Many people have found using Tarot cards to be effective for them. This is why I wanted to cover a chapter on using cards. I have a set of Tarot cards for readings that I bought about a year ago, after finally connecting with a pack that just seemed easy to read. You will know what I mean when you find your own set of cards, if this is to be your method of undertaking personal readings. You *do* have to be psychic, or clairvoyant to some degree, in order to read Tarot cards, because it's all about honing your senses to gather information which is not physical proof.

Tarot cards have been used for hundreds of years and can be traced back as far as 1440, when they first appeared in Italy. Originally a game created for nobles, the original deck was called Visconti Trumps and they also appeared soon after 1440 in France. They have been used for prediction by mystics and such- like for a long time and are still very popular today. When Jody suggested using Tarot cards one evening in our development circle my immediate response was one of panic. This was not because they are meant to have occult connotations, but because I didn't have the faintest idea of how to read them. I had bought a deck of cards a few years ago because they were the 'in thing' at the time, but I had quickly become bored with them. I found there were too many cards to remember the meanings of. The pack came with an instruction book on how to 'read' each of the 72 cards together with the meaning of each card. I remember looking at the instruction book and wondering how I was meant to learn all of the meanings and apply them to individual people. I soon gave up on the idea and the deck of cards gathered dust on a book shelf for several years. So when we discussed using cards in our development circle, I remembered that I had a deck tucked away somewhere and dug them out.

When we came to our development group that night, we all sat round in anticipation, wondering just how we were going to give Tarot readings without any knowledge of what the cards meant. We were divided into twos and asked that one be a reader and the other the recipient, or 'querient'. We were to give the cards to the querient to shuffle and to divide the pack into three piles. We would then ask them to choose one pile out of the three; the reader would then turn over the first three cards of that pile. The first card would be representing the past, the next card representing the present time and the last card to represent six months into the future.

I was paired up with a young girl and we started with me being the reader. I used a pack of Oracle cards, which basically has an image on each card with one word above it which would be significant. The first card showed a lotus flower with the word 'Unfoldment', which to me signified a person who was just beginning to blossom. I started to give my reading and found that the words came quite easily. It was nothing too startling at all to begin with, but suddenly, out of the blue, I had an image of her father and I felt that he was distant in location from her. She said that Dad was actually living in America, at which point other images began popping into my head. I had the impression of a girl who was in-between work, but then I saw an image of a desk and I knew this was something relevant to studying. She told me that she thought she had failed to get into university, so had found herself a job that she didn't particularly like, only to later discover that a few weeks earlier she had in fact got into university and so was unsure as to what to do. She felt she would go back to studying again, but was in the process of deciding. I then had the image of a young man, who was clearly her boyfriend and a very on and off relationship. I could tell she was easily frustrated with him at times and at other times loved him dearly. He felt significant to her at that time, but was someone who she would possibly move on from. It was a strange feeling as the cards were no longer significant. They were almost a prop to start a conversation. They weren't inaccurate but they were just a very small part of the reading; more of a focal point to look at whilst the main information came through.

The girl then read for me and used her pack of Tarot cards. I shuffled them for her and divided the pack into three and chose a pile. The young girl, Lottie, turned over my three cards and looked at the first one for my past. She looked down at the card for a little while and drew a complete blank. The image on it was of a man in robes, which neither of us recognised, 'The Hierophant'. I looked as blank as she did; neither of us knew what this card was meant to signify. We looked up the meaning in the instruction book. It said that the hierophant is a spiritual leader, who shares his divine knowledge to bring the community together and to lead his flock. He provides a link between heaven and Earth, but he also has great power over others which can be used for manipulation. In simple terms - if you can imagine the Pope with a sly and devious side, then this card would be him! It can refer to organised religion and also how we fit into the structure of the world. It can also refer to those people who control us, or try to control us. This was not mentioned in the book; this was something that I discovered later on. Lottie asked me if a religious person had influenced my earlier years, to which I said 'no'. However, if I took away the religious part of the meaning, then I could see that it would refer to a particularly controlling man in my childhood, who fitted the bill exactly. He was an abusive man who had to be loved by all around him. He was the life and soul of the party and a violent and vile man behind closed doors. Unfortunately both Lottie and I were concentrating so hard on trying to work out the exact meaning of the card that we overlooked any information she was getting by using her instincts or spirit guide. It was almost as if she was too afraid to say what she thought because she might get it totally wrong, or because I may react badly to what she really thought. Looking at it from her point of view, it would be quite intimidating for a young woman to discuss something that looked like it could be upsetting for someone she barely knew. I know full well if I was about 20years old, I would be terrified of saying to a woman who was nearly twice my age that she'd had an awful childhood with an abusive stepfather. What if I got it wrong? The woman may react really badly! This is exactly what was going through Lottie's head and why she tentatively gave me the odd bit of information and then stopped.

After 20 minutes we all moved on to another person within the group to see what information we got on our second time round. This was when I made a big discovery. I asked the lady I was with this time to give the cards a shuffle just as before and divide the pack into three. Again I turned over the first three cards as before and looked at them. I remember clearly seeing the middle card, for the present, which showed a stormy sea, black clouds and lightning striking the rocks. The word written underneath was 'Power' and I recall starting the reading talking about that particular card, as I felt this was most significant. I looked at the word and began talking about how I thought she was getting power back somehow and that up until now things had been bad for her. I had the strong feeling that this was a very dark period in her life and that it had suddenly come to head. The more I dismissed the word 'Power' and went with what I was feeling, the stronger my instincts became. I knew that this was a very low time for her, but felt that it would pass very quickly. Looking at her future card it was very positive. It showed a beautiful scene of mountains and water looking through a crystal cave, and the word above it was 'Focus'.

As I started to talk again about regaining her focus and how positive the future was, I felt that the word was sending me in the wrong direction again and once more I went with what I was feeling. I could see changes in a job, a house move and many positive new things. I also had an overwhelming tingling sensation in my head, which is my indicator that a spirit is present, and I clearly felt a man standing right next to me. At this point I said to the lady that I felt the spirit of a man was with her and straight away I got the message that this was her father. He had his head held low, as if in shame. I received the clear message that he was sorry and so I gave this message to her. I could clearly sense that her childhood had been quite unhappy and that her mother had tried to compensate for the lack of love and attention she never received from her father. She then told me that, yes, her childhood had been unhappy; that life was currently very chaotic with a house move and job change and that she had suffered a miscarriage that week. I felt extremely sad for this lady's loss, but as soon as I told her how sad I was to hear that, I had the overwhelming sensation of a bouncing little boy with her. I could see him as clear as crystal in my mind, with straight fair hair and chubby cheeks, a beautiful little chap. I passed this message on to her and she told me that another medium had predicted a baby boy for the following year, too. She then left on a very positive note as we wrapped up the reading.

This taught me a huge lesson in that sometimes you have to go with what you feel is right and not what is written. Anybody can perform a reading using Tarot/Angel or Oracle cards, simply by using a book that gives you the meanings. However, a good medium will use the cards as a focus and interpret their own meaning, which is not necessarily what has been written down. I have heard of several mediums that literally use a regular pack of playing cards. They do not refer to the writings of an instruction book, but instead use the cards to focus the information. The cards are not wrong in their meaning as such, but are more of a guideline. If you think about it, how can one specific 'meaning' apply to each and every person? There have to be variations depending on the querient. It would be like stating that all people with the same illness are exactly alike. Just as we are all unique and we all have unique interpretations, it requires a good medium to give a fuller and more accurate reading. They will use their clairvoyant and psychic abilities, not just read from an instruction book.

After this session I went home and got out my husband's small pots of acrylic paint, which he uses for work and painted out all of the words in my cards. I spent about two hours matching up each colour on the heading, so it matched the rest of the card and they looked the same. I knew at this point that I was so dedicated to what I was doing, that nothing was going to stand in the way of my spiritual growth. Once you get to this stage, when you are so obsessed with what you are doing that you dedicate most of your time to it, I think you can assume that you are on the right path! This was the moment that I had been craving. I knew at last that I had an ability that I could work with, and I would eventually be coming out of the spiritual closet.

There is a lot of superstition connected with Tarot cards, so I want briefly to dispel some of the hype. Tarot cards are NOT connected to the devil or any form of black/dark magic. I personally think that this theory is absolute mystical rubbish, used to make people feel more important or to fear them. Any worthwhile medium will be grounded, down- to- Earth and possess a huge dose of common sense! Witchcraft in itself has been hyped up by the media to be something associated with evil and devilment. Again, I think this is total rubbish in most cases! Witchcraft, if you look at its origins is more to do with using herbs to heal, appreciating the energy of the Earth and all living things. In simple terms, it's an appreciation of nature and our living planet. A witch, who practises witchcraft for the good of others, is deemed a guardian of the Earth; someone who seeks a balanced life with plants, animals, seasons, and the Earth itself. They should not be feared, but emulated if anything! It's estimated that witchcraft goes back thousands of years to pre-historic times, where paintings have been found by archaeologists in caves. The association to the occult slowly built up over the years, through superstition and misinformation. The word 'occult' itself originates from the Latin term 'occultus' meaning secret, hidden from view, or concealed. This, over time, has been associated with dark magic and devil worship, rather than the simple truth which was more likely to refer to a shrewd woman, who was handy with a few herbs and the use of psychology!

<u>Exercise 6 – Reading Cards</u>

There is a huge amount of myth and ritual attached to reading Tarot cards. I think, to be honest, that it's totally unnecessary. All die-hard Tarot readers will be getting the kindling ready for me again. However, I am going to stick my neck on the line here and say what I think is more accurate. The method below is how I was taught and it works for me beautifully. If it didn't work, I wouldn't be writing about it and my tutor would not have taught it either. So on that note, I will let you decide for yourself. Give it a go yourself and see what you think.

Start by picking out a set of cards to use. Choosing the right Tarot deck can be like finding the right partner, so it may take time to connect with a deck. When I looked at my first deck of cards, the images were really hard for me to connect with, despite the fact that they are renowned for being a favourite deck amongst many Tarot readers. Instead, I looked for a pack that appealed to me and since finding a deck that I can connect with I have never looked back. I use them for all of my personal readings now and wouldn't be without them.

Many people have said that you have to be given a deck of cards as a gift and that you should never buy your own. The main problem there is that the cards have to connect with you on a personal level, plus someone has to actually buy a set for you. I found personally that as soon as I saw my Tarot cards, they just felt right. They were bright and beautifully coloured, just like paintings. I find them exceptionally easy to read, whereas someone else may hate them and get little from them. There are numerous decks available in shops or on-line so it should be easy to choose one that connects with you. The images should almost speak to you like a work of art. In the same way that certain sculptures or paintings stir up feelings within us, your cards should evoke the same feelings. This will not be the same for all of us as different people resonate with different decks. Once you have your cards they will almost become part of you if you are meant to use them as a form of communicating. Some people wrap their deck in silk, velvet, or satin, but to be honest it is really up to you. If you are the sort of person that loves anything Egyptian, then a gorgeous stone box encased in hieroglyphs may be perfect. If you prefer more of a mystical theme, then choose an ornately carved box or embroidered pouch. I keep mine in a black velvet bag that I made myself and feel that there is a little bit of me surrounding my deck. However, as long as you treat them well and keep them safe they will treat you well, too.

When you have your cards, start to get to know them and see how they make you feel. Have them with you as much as possible and start by looking at your own life using the three card timeline of past, present and future and see what you get. Does it look accurate to you? Alternatively, shuffle the cards and think of a question you would like answered. Turn over one card (or three for a fuller answer) and see which card you get by way of an answer. You should be able to tell if the message is positive or negative at the very least. Do remember that lottery wins etc. are not likely to be predicted. Your spiritual development is exactly that, spiritual! It's not so much about predicting the future or Earthly concerns such as 'is my partner going to marry me?' That is for *you* to decide, not spirit. They will instead give you guidance for the future and can foretell of babies very accurately (no idea why!). If used for reading other people, you should be able to tell a lot about the person you have in front of you and the life they have had. Some cards may not mean anything to you or just feel wrong; if this is the case then dismiss them. I know most Tarot readers will be horrified at this, but until you can associate a meaning there is little point in trying to guess inaccurately at one. You may find that the querient gives you information that helps establish the meaning over time, but whilst you are learning don't feel pressurised to guess a meaning. You may end up getting it totally wrong and losing confidence in your abilities. If you feel confident enough to make an established prediction, then do so. Try not to be put off if it's not quite right, the main idea is that you learn what your cards are telling you over time.

Something in the future may be clear to see, such as someone considering a new job for example, or a change in career. However, the cards are not there to tell a person what to do, they just predict it as a strong possibility, unless action is taken to steer them onto a different course. So should you see an impending divorce or similar bad news, you should not tell the person that this is definitely going to happen. Instead, say that you can see the marriage is quite unsteady and that it may end in divorce, unless the two of them work at their relationship together. Please be tactful about how you deliver your messages if they are not overly positive.

The more you use your cards or just hold/shuffle them, the more of your 'energy' will be imprinted on them. I would not advise you let anyone use them for their own readings, but you can certainly 'cleanse' them should this occur. This is the advice given by Steven Farmer who produces the Earth Magic Oracle cards.

"Examine each card individually and then hold the whole deck over your heart with the images facing you. Have your feet firmly on the ground and close your eyes. Take three deep breaths and ask for your spirit guide to help you clearly interpret the meanings of your cards and to fill them with blessings. Take another deep breath and focus your intention whilst gently blowing into your cards."

To undertake a reading for someone else it's better to try on someone you know very little about if possible, so that you can check if the information you feel you are receiving is accurate. This is preferable to basing it on someone you know well where you already know a lot about them. Try to perform a reading in a quiet place where it is calm and peaceful, in the same way as you would do for clairvoyance. It helps to quieten the mind first so that you are more receptive to the information you receive. Similarly to the way that you pick up any information from other people, the cards will almost speak to you when you use them. The information you receive should be felt instinctively, so use all of your senses to gather information. If a certain card makes you feel uncomfortable, try to analyse why and in what way. Does it make you feel frustrated, afraid, nervous or sad? Trust these emotions more than the information that is written in a guide book. All psychic and clairvoyant abilities rely mainly on their ability to sense. The more you practise and trust the information you feel, the better you will become.

If you find you are simply not getting anything at all, then do not force it. It may simply not be your chosen technique. Whatever method you use for clairvoyance, it should feel 'right' and eventually become effortless and instinctive. So if after several attempts you are not connecting with your cards, it may be that the actual cards themselves are not right for you, or that the actual method itself is not right for you.

One lady in our group studied the meanings of her deck diligently only to find when she gave her reading to the man, her querient, he didn't relate to any of it at all. In fact he found that the opposite was true for much of the information she gave or that it had no relation to him at all. Once Jody asked the lady to go with what she felt and guided her on what she, as an established reader, felt the meanings were, the reading was accurate and completely different from the original message. The lady concerned was so cross with herself because she had spent so much time learning the supposed meaning behind each card. After that she said that she was buying a new deck of cards as soon as possible. She would not be using that deck again because she now associated them with all of the meanings she had learnt.

I originally started using Oracle cards which, though beautiful, were not detailed enough for me. There was an array of positive messages and meanings, but only a small handful of negative meanings. Unfortunately a lot of people who came to me for a reading had many issues that they were trying to deal with. This is quite often the case with people requesting readings. If everything was marvellous they would have little need of a medium. When I moved over to a set of Tarot cards, I found my readings to be far more accurate. There were a lot more negatives than in my original Oracle cards and they depicted people which I would interpret as people in the querient's life. One lady asked if she could do me a reading as she was learning and wanted to be able to attach some meanings to her set of cards. She was using Oracle cards which had beautiful images with words above, similar to those I had previously used. I shuffled them for her and handed them back to her so she could lay them out in three lines showing my past, present and future. As her cards depicted scenes and were on the whole mostly positive, it was very hard for her to see anything but the positive side of my life to date and my future according to the cards was absolutely fantastic! It was a lovely reading, which though great for my future, was difficult for her to read accurately for my past. Unfortunately, she could not pick up a lot about my past at all, which had been really quite dire, as her cards were so positive. The few negative cards that were in the pack all came up in my past, but they depicted scenes rather than people so my reader struggled to give a detailed reading. When she did another reading for me using a set of Tarot cards instead, her reading was far more accurate and she was able to pick out certain people in my past. There was a card showing a fierce warrior on horseback, who looked like an Ork from the film *Lord of the Rings*. Not a nice chap at all; quite different from the man who appeared on another card in my early past, who she had established was my Dad. She knew this 'warrior' man in my past had caused a great deal of upset and hurt for me from the image shown. She then established that if it was not Dad, it was more than likely a step-father, as there were no other males in my childhood. She was of course spot on and although the Tarot guidebook gave a different interpretation to the one she gave, hers was far better. When she said what she felt, rather than what was written in the book, her reading was far more precise.

When I bought my Tarot cards I never learnt any of the meanings as defined in the Tarot guidebook. If doing a reading I would set them out in three rows of seven cards to a row, for past, present and future. I would ask the querient to shuffle them, but not turn any upside down as is traditional. I would literally just describe what I felt the cards were telling me from my instincts, not what the book stated. I also found that certain cards always meant exactly the same thing for every person who came for a reading, whereas other cards were open to interpretation. There is one card in the Tarot deck (8 of swords), which shows a blindfolded woman with rope wrapped around her middle. This card always means a miscarriage or a termination and so far it has never been wrong. The Tower card always means a divorce or separation and another, (5 of wands), shows a man in a circle with a stick, fending off other men in the circle who also have sticks. This always indicates a family argument. All of these cards have the same meaning for me whenever I do a reading and will give me my anchor points which I can work from. Some cards I struggled to interpret at first, or felt wrong, so I ignored them. It's good to remember that just because a card has been put down, you do not have to read it if it feels wrong or you are unsure. I know this may be a little difficult to understand, but you will have more of an idea when you actually try to do a reading. Say what you feel and read the cards intuitively and you should be on the right lines. In time they will begin to make sense and all will have a meaning for you

It's worth remembering that you need cards which have some negatives on them to be able to do a more accurate reading, but most importantly to pick a set that you resonate with.

Chapter 7: Why do we Get it Wrong?

If I had a pound for every time I was asked this question, I would be a very rich woman! Some of the reasons why we get it wrong have been covered in chapters 5 & 6, which basically state that we cannot know everything because it would be too easy. Spirit does not come armed with every scrap of information in advance, instead they use our memory bank of feelings and memories. It's about being confident enough to trust in those feelings.

I cannot emphasise enough that clairvoyance does not work like having a conversation in which you are told lots of details. It will be more like having thoughts that are not your own. The more you relax and let it flow, the more your clairvoyance will flow. If you are sitting or standing there saying, 'I cannot get anything, come on give me something', the harder it will be for you to receive any information, which is immensely frustrating. It's almost like the harder you try, the less you get. When you take your time and do not panic, you will almost absorb the emotions and energy being given to you and it will seem as if the information is obvious. There will be some things that you feel you are absolutely right about and when you get a 'no' back from a person you will feel confused because it feels like it should be right. Do not take the information back – you would have been given that information for a reason. I will try to illustrate some reasons why it may have been deemed as wrong.

Misinterpretation – A lot of messages come through in the form of symbols or memories, which will mean something to us as the medium, but not necessarily the person who we are reading for. One lady in our group, 'Tina', was connecting to a spirit and had an uncomfortable feeling in her stomach, when asking how the spirit had died. She then had the image of a car crash pop into her mind. The lady she was reading for identified that her grandfather had died of a stomach cancer, but could not understand the car crash message. Tina checked again and asked if this was right. Again she had the pain in her stomach and then she saw a car crash. The car was hurtling along at a great speed and then it suddenly crashed and everything went black. She described to the lady what she had felt, saying that it seemed so sudden, and that she kept getting the same images. The lady then said her grandfather's cancer was extremely sudden and that he died literally days after being diagnosed. This then began to make sense and Tina now finds when she is given the images of the sudden car crash, she knows the death of the person was sudden and unexpected.

Many messages that come through need to be deciphered just as this one did, so it may take a while to build up your library of images, symbols and sensations. Once you have deciphered a meaning, try to remember the images or feelings you associated with it, as it will more than likely be used again. Another example could be that you are shown the image of a big red double-decker bus. Think of what this could mean? It could mean that your spirit was a bus driver, unlikely, but certainly possible. It can refer to travelling, either that the spirit was prone to travelling or that the person you are reading for will be travelling somewhere. It could refer to a London bus; it could be that spirit was from London or that there is a London connection to the person you are reading for. There are often many different meanings associated with some objects. It is difficult to start with. Just bear in mind that in the beginning you will need to interpret or decipher your information before getting it right each time.

If you are unsure about what you are being told, ask your spirit guide to help you decipher the meaning. It's okay to be firm with your guide and ask for a more specific message. If you do not tell your guide that you would like further information, then you won't get it. Think of it as going back to school. If you don't tell the teacher that you need more details in order to understand, then they won't give them to you.

Denial – Now this aspect is a difficult one, because you may find that the person you are reading for does not want to accept the information you are giving, even if you are 99.99% sure that you are right. They may say, for example, that Mum was always a happy person who loved doing everything for her family. You, however, may be getting the message that Mum was actually a person who was taken advantage of and often felt unappreciated. These conflicting messages can be difficult to prove either way, so if this happens move on to another subject or message.

Do not be tempted to prove that you are right and argue the fact, as you may cause a lot of upset. Some people are not ready to hear that their nearest and dearest were not happy when alive so will stay in denial. You should not push people into changing their minds, if they are sure they are right. It's better to gloss over the subject and say that you may have misinterpreted the message, or something similar. It can be difficult when someone has passed on and when faced with the truth, either about their loved ones or themselves, the living can carry a lot of guilt or denial. They can completely shut down and categorically argue that you have your information wrong.

Interference – Sometimes communicating can be difficult purely down to a poor connection. It's like tuning into a radio station where you may get a lot of 'static', with only some bits that are clear. You can ask for information to be repeated, but on occasions you just won't be able to get a clear signal. This can be down to a number of different reasons pertaining to you, spirit, or the person you reading for.

If you are unwell, or not fully relaxed, then this will make the connection weaker. The same goes for the person you are reading for. If they are very negative to the idea of clairvoyance or are not open with you, it can make the reading very difficult. The information will come through, but you may have to work at it! If a person arrives with their arms crossed and barely says a word to you, or deliberately goes out of their way to be difficult, it may be worth calling a halt to the reading.

There is nothing worse than struggling to get a connection for someone who is deliberately awkward, or for someone who does not actually want to be there. You may wonder why on Earth they would even come in the first place, but trust me, it happens occasionally. Interference could also be down to the fact that the spirit does not connect well with you as a person. If you are trying to communicate with a spirit, for example, who spent her life hating men and you happen to be a male medium, then she may not feel comfortable talking to you. If the spirit was a very private person who rarely spoke to people, you may find that they still do not like communicating and that you only get snippets of information that are not very clear. I recently read for a lady, who had her sister- in -law with her. Her father came through and was a very quiet man. When reading for her it felt like I was extracting teeth and the information came through so slowly, it almost had to be drawn out. I finished the reading eventually and all was well, but it took a lot of work. I then spoke to her again about three hours later when we were alone and her father came through so clearly I thought I was being electrocuted with tingles! He was so connected to me; it was almost like being with a different man. As he was a quiet man, the message he wanted to give was private and for her alone. It's only with experience that you will learn what works best.

Interference can also mean that you do not hear or interpret the message clearly, a bit like Chinese whispers. There was a great example of this during WW1 where one of the most famous cases of mishearing a message occurred. The original message from the trenches to British HQ was "Send reinforcements, we're going to advance". This was interpreted as "Send three and four pence, we're going to a dance." So you can see how difficult it can be for living people to communicate, let alone those who are in spirit!

Deliberate misinformation – Imagine you had done something which you felt deeply ashamed of, or guilty about. For example, imagine you had given up a child, or that you had abused your husband or wife and then you had died. You would carry that shame or guilt with you when you passed on. Just because you are in spirit does not suddenly make you free of all negative emotions. Now imagine that someone connected to you wants to make contact with you, but you do not want to. It may be that you would not communicate at all, or that you would give the medium misleading information to compensate for your guilt. It's the same principle with living people. Some children are told that Mum or Dad has died or moved away, rather than being told, for example, that they are in prison.   Some people tell lies in order to 'protect' their family from the truth. I am not convinced this is the right thing to do, but I can understand why some people feel the need to do so. The same principle can work in spirit. A spirit may deliberately give misinformation for one reason or another. I don't think it's very common, but I do believe it can happen.

The lesson – Sometimes we need to be brought back down to Earth. It can be that we are too stressed, or that we take our gift for granted, or some other reason. Either way, it has been decided that you need time out from your spiritual communication and your gift may be taken back for a while. I have heard several mediums talk about a period of not being able to make good connections, or having a run of poor readings when usually they have been very accurate. I believe that this is a lesson for us to not take our gift for granted, or that we need to make time for ourselves. When we are at our best, our readings will also be at their best, so sometimes we need to take time out and recharge our own batteries. Do not underestimate how beneficial it is to have some 'you' time!

Wonky aerial – Quite often in our development circle, we would sit there trying to connect to someone and we would feel a spirit come through. We would then connect it to someone within the circle. We would make the connection and start a reading for that person. On occasions they would look back at us with blank faces because they could not relate to any of the message. This would be quite confusing.

Nine times out of ten the reading was actually for someone sitting nearby and it all made perfect sense to them! Quite often you will find that if a person brings a friend along for a reading, you may find information coming through for the friend as well as the person you are meant to be reading for. Spirits are attracted to mediums like moths to a light bulb! They are not concerned if you are reading for the right person or not, all they know is that you can hear them and they are going to make darned sure that they speak to you! When you tune in for clairvoyance, it's like shining a massive beam of light into the spirit world and those with the loudest voices tend to come through first.

It may be that you have several spirits come at the same time. I have known times when I have picked up on two spirits at once for two different people, which can be very confusing. It does take a little time to sort out your spiritual aerial so that you know who you are working with. Some mediums when working on a larger scale, such as on stage, will connect to spirit and throw it open to a group of people. It's not that they're hedging their bets, it's just that it would take forever to go through each person in the audience. It's also the case that you will find some spirits are very eager to get through and come through quickly and clearly, whilst others will be a little quieter and may come through nearer the end of a reading.

Nightmares with names – I have often found that I get several names of people spot on whilst others are not known to the person I am reading for. That can be the one aspect that can make or break a reading. When it's right, you have captivated the person you are reading for, but when it's wrong they can switch right off. Try not to get hung up on names as you will be sensing the names of someone for a reason. It may be someone relevant to the spirit; it may be that you have misheard the name or simply that you have another spirit calling out, or that the spirit reminds you of someone with the same name. If you feel comfortable say it anyway, but I wouldn't worry too much, as when you try describing the spirit you will find the information flows much better. I tend to either get the name or the first letter of the name which somehow feels right. For example, when you are connected to spirit and briefly go through the alphabet, a letter or two will feel right to you and will be associated to the spirit you are connected to. When you think of any other letter, you know it doesn't feel right. I had a wonderful example a little while ago when I was reading for a gentleman. I was connected to the spirit of his wife and I had been given the letters M-A-Y when talking to her. I then asked the gentleman if his wife was called May. He shook his head and said to me that he didn't know a May, so I focused again and still got the same letters. He still looked at me blankly so I moved on. I said that it felt as though he and his wife had two children, a boy and a girl, and he said that yes they did, but that their daughter was in spirit. The daughter's name was Amy just like mine. It then clicked as to why I was seeing those letters. His wife was trying to tell me that she was with their daughter. I knew then that I had heard the letters correctly, I just had them in the wrong order. If this does happen, make a note of the letters you are feeling and try putting them in a different order. Alternatively, give the letters to the person you are reading for and you may find that they can place them.

They just don't know – Sometimes you will get a message for someone where you are absolutely spot-on with your information, but the person you are reading for just cannot make the connection. I had the exact same experience myself when being on the other side of the fence as it were. I was having a reading myself where the medium, Paul, had connected to my Dad. Paul gave me information that, at the time, I didn't know what he was referring to and thought he had it wrong. It was only later, after speaking to my husband that we joined up the dots and noted that Paul had in fact got it completely right. Another lady who was practising her clairvoyance on me in our development circle mentioned that she could see a large golden Labrador that had come to say hello. I told her I had two dogs, both living, but that they were quite small. One is golden and white, a West Highland Terrier cross, which looks like a Labrador puppy and the other is grey and tan. She checked again and started to change her mind, but then finally stuck to her guns and said that she was certain it was a Labrador. She said he was quite an old, slow dog with a slightly saggy tummy and that he was very friendly. She described how he was resting his head in my lap and that he had dropped a shoe on the floor. I suddenly recalled a good friend of mine who'd had a large golden Labrador that had died a few weeks before. He always would come over when I visited and would rest his head on my lap, so I could stroke his head and rub under his chin. He was an adorable dog and extremely missed by his family. It looked like 'Harry' wanted to drop in and say hello. I was so pleased that he had, as I, too, was very sad when he passed over. At the time I was so busy trying to make my own dogs 'fit' what the lady was seeing, that I hadn't even thought about the possibility of a different dog coming to say hello. This can be very common when reading for someone, so rather than retract your statement, stick to your original thoughts. If the person still cannot make the link then ask them to make a note of what you are saying and to take that away with them. Sometimes statements you give to people only become apparent over time, so do not be afraid to say what you see or feel.

Exercise 7 – Reading for Someone New

As I've said, the only way you are going to be able to progress is by reading for someone you do not know very well. I appreciate this can be tricky, but you will need to be able to practise your skills on someone. If you are not part of a development circle, or spiritual church, you are going to have to find yourself a willing victim! There are development circles, which can also be found on-line, where you can practise your skills with others who are practising, too. Don't be put off by the fact that the person is on-line. Each person there is a beginner and will share your trepidation. You will all be in the same boat, as it were, so try to overcome your nerves and just have a go. Spirit does not mind connecting to you wherever you are, just as long as you are comfortable and willing to have a go. It's better if you are in front of someone, but you can certainly receive a lot of information from photographs and practise over the internet. I still work on-line with photographs now and find my readings are just as accurate.

Try to calm your mind first before 'tuning in' to spirit, or if you prefer to, meditate first and then go on- line. As long as you are comfortable and relaxed, you should be able to get something. Go through a check list of questions to ask the spirit as a guideline, if you get stuck for information. The most important point to remember is to 'Say it and sod it!' When you are learning nobody is going to expect you to get it right every time, so don't worry. I can guarantee that if you have got some of your information wrong, you will not be the first person to do so, or most certainly the last.

The more often you practise your clairvoyance, the better you will become. Just like learning a foreign language, if you put it into practice you will find it easier over time, and the same is true for clairvoyance. The most crucial piece of advice I would give to you is to trust the information you are receiving, even though it will be very subtle. You may become panicked early on that you are not getting much information. I did this a lot in my early days, but when you start talking about a spirit, you will find more and more snippets of information coming through as you continue to talk.

Guidance Tips

As I said previously, the best piece of guidance I can give is to keep asking questions of the spirit you are connected to, and to give 100% of the information that you are receiving. I found occasionally that I would still hold back a little bit and doubt the information that I was getting. I'd then kick myself when the person I would be reading for would tell me about the spirit when they were alive and I would find that I had known it all along. Sometimes you will want to be able to prove that you are right so badly that you end up too afraid of getting it wrong.

As a previous teacher, I would absolutely hate getting anything wrong. When teaching I was relied upon to give accurate information and trusted to know what I was talking about. Developing my clairvoyance was the biggest leap of faith, quite literally, that I had ever undertaken! I had to rely on feelings, images and thoughts that would pop into my head, which was not the most reliable way of passing information to others. Personally, getting something wrong felt like the world was about to end; I hated not having anything definite to work with. It was not something I was comfortable with at all and I would feel my confidence sinking unless every scrap of information was 100% accurate. The worst thing about this was that I needed to practise and get it wrong, in order to progress. I found that the more I practised the better I became, so it really was a case of having to bite the bullet. If you find yourself worrying in the same way about looking a complete fool or getting it wrong, I can honestly say we all go through it and it is part of the learning process. Even the best mediums will have got something wrong at some point, or slightly misinterpreted a piece of information. They all learned from it though and carried on to be successful in their abilities. If it was any other profession you were learning, would you expect to get everything right within the first six months or so? If you treat this as you would any other profession and give yourself time, you will develop your skills more effectively. You may also find that if you are changing spirit guides that you go through a period of quiet. Again, this is quite normal.

You may start by getting images drop into your mind which you need to interpret. So if the person you are reading for looks puzzled or says 'no' to you, try to look at it from another perspective. One lady who was just starting to learn clairvoyance, kept seeing a small cottage in the middle of nowhere when she began reading for people. It was an image that cropped up in several readings that the recipient couldn't place and she couldn't understand. When she stopped and thought how the image made her feel, she had one of those 'Eureka' moments. She said that the cottage looks very isolated and a bit of a lonely place; it didn't feel like a happy cottage because it was entirely on its own and almost empty. When she applied this meaning to the spirit she was connected to, she was absolutely 100% accurate. The spirit when alive had been a very lonely person, someone who had felt quite isolated from everyone else. It's often worth looking at images from a different view point in order to ascertain the real meaning. Each time she sees the same image of the cottage now, she knows that the spirit she is connected to would have led quite a lonely life and felt cut off from the people around them. This will be the case for you, too. Once you have established what an image or feeling means to you, trust it, as I can almost guarantee it will mean the same each and every time.

Remember this is about you developing that relationship and learning how your guide will communicate to you. In the early days you are not going to know immediately what to expect or how they will pass information. Over time you will get the same images, feelings and sensations that you will recognise and be able to interpret. It is really, really subtle! I cannot stress this enough, but once you are aware of it in the future it won't feel subtle to you, you will know what it means.

"I have not failed;
I have just found 10,000 ways that didn't work."

Thomas Eddison

Chapter 8: Roots, Tree Hugging and Chocolate

Grounding yourself is a very important part of clairvoyance. If you don't ground yourself after clairvoyance, you will be leaving yourself constantly open to spirit and possibly have Uncle Tom Cobley and all dropping in. You will also feel like you are getting over an illness where it leaves you drained and feeling not quite your usual self.

When you connect to the spirit world, you are tuning in to another plane, and many mediums feel that they are not quite here in the 'real world' anymore. It's hard to describe really because it's not like we actually see anything different. We are, however, in a different 'Zone'. It's very similar to being so engrossed in something, that you are totally unaware of what is going on around you. You are there physically, but mentally you are 100% focused on what you are doing. This level of concentration can leave you feeling really drained and often give you a splitting headache. Clairvoyance, unfortunately, can be the same and many people who practise their clairvoyance often complain of headaches, tiredness and nausea at times. The closest thing I can compare it to is altitude sickness, where the air has less oxygen. Those who have been mountaineering, skiing or snowboarding will know what I am talking about here.

In my early days of going to my development circle, myself and several others members, would suffer from headaches at the end of the session when we went home. Some of them left me feeling like I wanted to crawl into a dark room and feel sorry for myself. I would also find that each time I connected fully to spirit, I would know instantly because I felt really quite sick. The stronger they came through, the sicker I felt. I still felt a massive amount of tingles in the back of my head, but I would feel nauseous and a bit 'spaced out', too. It sounds fabulous doesn't it? I can say, however, that now I'm communicating with spirit more regularly it has become a lot easier and I rarely get nauseous at all, unless it's connected with the health of the spirit. I do feel a little light- headed at times, which is not so bad, and I find that grounding after clairvoyance helps this feeling to pass.

Now I can imagine you are sitting there reading this thinking, 'Why would I want to develop my clairvoyance if it makes you feel that lousy?' Well I can't guarantee solutions to take away all symptoms, but I can certainly suggest things that are well worth a try and should help.

When you begin to connect to spirit, make a note of how you feel in yourself. If you find that you are feeling unwell when you connect, start by connecting for brief periods initially. Ten minutes to half an hour at the most would be a good starting place. Then if you feel well in yourself, you can build up the connection period over time. Also if the connection is really strong, and leaves you feeling 'spaced out' and nauseous, ask for the spirit to come through more gently. You can also ask your spirit guide to lessen the connection for you. Don't worry, you will still get all of the information you need, just without feeling unwell. In the early days of learning I used to feel really terrible, but now I just feel light- headed if the connection is strong.

When you have finished a clairvoyant session, make sure you ground yourself. Read through Exercise 8 below and see which of the methods work best for you. When you forget to do this, you won't notice anything big or dramatic, but you may find that you start picking up on other spirits who just happen to drop in. This happened once when I was communicating with spirit and the phone rang. I completely forgot to ground myself and then went out shopping for groceries. Whilst I was out, I felt like I had the spirits of everybody's long - lost relatives dropping in for me to pass messages to. This was not ideal when deciding what chicken to buy! I came home and felt like I was absolutely drained; almost like being drunk or drugged. I had the same feeling when I was taking strong medication following surgery. My husband asked me if I had grounded myself recently, as he had been very aware of my periods of nausea becoming more frequent, to which I looked down at my feet and mumbled, 'no, I had been busy and forgot'. So after a brief chastisement we both went outside for a walk with our dogs and I felt much better. I reminded myself that next time I really would have to make a conscious effort to remember to ground myself fully. Bear in mind when you open yourself up to the spirit world, it's like shining a torch out on their plane and you resemble a human lighthouse. If you forget to turn the light off, it does not stop shining out to everyone, even if *you* feel that you are not open for business.

Being grounded means that you are solidly fixed and connected to your 'Earthly' surroundings again and you will be safe, calm and totally aware of all going on around you. When you are not grounded, you may feel unable to focus or concentrate and you risk being influenced by the energy and emotions around you.

Exercise 8 – Grounding Yourself

There are different ways in which to ground yourself, which we have covered briefly before in other chapters, but we will go over in more detail here. Read through each one below and find a method that works for you.

Roots – It's always a good idea to have your feet planted flat on the ground, when either connecting to spirit, or meditating. When you have finished your reading, you can stay sitting down or you can stand up. Just ensure that your feet are still flat on the ground. Always thank your guide for working with you, as again this is easily forgotten, but polite to do so. Also thank the person who has come to you for a reading, thus ending your reading on a positive note. When ready, imagine your feet are slowly growing roots that are working their way into the ground. Picture all of your clairvoyant and psychic energy, flowing out through your body and into the roots as they grow. If you prefer to visualise the spiritual energy as a colour, then do so. Just picture it flowing out of you from the top of your head down to your feet and draining into the roots. It should only take a minute or two. Just make sure you have imagined yourself empty of spiritual energy, so that all of your spiritual connection has flowed completely into the roots.

Some people find showering or washing their hands helps, rather than picturing roots coming out of their feet. They picture the shower as an energising shower that washes away the clairvoyant connection. This can work equally well; just make sure that the water is running water, rather than bathing water. If the water is bathing water, then you will have a whole tub full of spiritual water swishing around you, instead of letting it wash away. Alternatively, have a quick shower after your bath, so that you rinse away the connection.

Tree Hugging – Come on, you didn't really expect to have a spiritual book without a mention of tree hugging! I'm not suggesting that you race outside and grab hold of the nearest oak, however going outside can actually help to ground you. When you go outside it connects you with the world again and makes you feel more 'alive'. When you have not been outside for several days, you feel hemmed in and some people complain of getting 'cabin fever'.

If you can go for a brief walk, or just sit in your garden if you have one, then do so as this is a great way of grounding yourself. It's just a matter of reconnecting yourself with your Earthly surroundings and the usual hustle and bustle of life again. Even if you live in the most remote place imaginable, you are totally surrounded by all living things. This is quite often why people have to get out in the open air when contemplating big decisions, or coming to terms with something. When we are outside it engulfs us with life and energy – it's absolutely everywhere; from the grass beneath our feet, to the breeze sweeping through the leaves in the trees. Birds, insects and all manner of different creatures surround us each and every day, but we are closer to them when we are outside. When we are out in the open, it reminds us that in the bigger scheme of things, we are actually quite small. Thousands of people will probably have walked the same path as us in the past, quite literally, in most cases. So if you do see a big old oak tree and feel the sudden urge to give it a hug, I'm sure the tree won't mind too much. Besides, hugging has been proven scientifically to make you feel better.

Stones, Pebbles & Crystals – Just like being outside, stones and crystals are a bit like bringing a little of the outside in. Most of them are incredibly old and have been about for some years, making up a large part of our planet. As they are part of the Earth, it sort of makes sense that they would connect us back to it.

Crystals and stones have been used for healing for numerous years, each having its own quality and use in healing or divining. Many mediums carry small stones with them that they use specifically for grounding. Black, brown and red stones are often most popular. Some of the stones most commonly used for grounding are made of black or snowflake obsidian, onyx, dark tourmaline, agate or hematite. There are other stones or crystals that can be used. It's just a matter of finding a stone or crystal that appeals to you. I have a sphere of gold sheen black obsidian which works wonderfully well for me. I didn't walk into my nearest crystal shop and try out a whole range, I just found that this particular stone appealed to me when I looked at it. It looked like a wonderful swirling galaxy in the midst of a shiny black round stone, and I thought it looked beautiful. After communicating with spirit one day, I thought it was worth holding for 10minutes to see if it worked as a grounding stone. It was marvellous and I literally felt my headache drain away. I had no idea if it was purely psychological or not, I just know it worked for me and I've used it ever since. I must admit that I was always very sceptical about the use of crystals and stones for healing. However, having found that this method works for me, it now makes it difficult to be so doubtful. I am still a little unsure about the use of healing through stones and crystals, as it's an area I don't tend to use. However as long as my stone continues to work for me, I really don't mind!

If you would like to have a go at grounding yourself using a stone or crystal, you first need to find one that appeals to you. Once you are ready to ground yourself, find somewhere quiet to go and hold the stone in your hand. Imagine all of your clairvoyant energy flowing out of you and into the stone. Do this for a few minutes or longer. When you feel calm, alert, and connected back to your surroundings, you can stop holding on to it. Remember to wash or rinse your stone in clear running water once it has been used; this is to cleanse it of any negative or spiritual energy it has absorbed. This is a good instruction for using your stone and, though it may seem a little odd, it's always stated when using stones for spiritual purposes. Again, I have no idea if it makes any great difference. I just don't want to take the chance of mine not working effectively, so I rinse mine each time!

Here are some of the properties of common grounding stones which I have found quite interesting. There is no solid evidence that any of the below can be proven, but still may be worth considering if choosing a stone for grounding purposes:

Agate – Agate attracts strength and is used as protection from bad dreams, stress and energy depletion. It's one of the oldest stones used for its mystical properties in recorded history. It has also been used in jewellery since biblical times to ward against storms, of all things. Additionally, it was placed under the pillow to induce rich and abundant dreams. It's used for healing stomach disorders, but due to its protective qualities, it is a common grounding stone.

Onyx – Onyx gives strength and promotes energy, commitment and endurance. It imparts self-confidence and helps you to be at ease in any surroundings. Onyx banishes grief, enhances self-control and stimulates the power of wisdom when decision-making. It's said to encourage happiness and good fortune. Onyx is often used to treat disorders of the bones, bone marrow and blood and is, apparently, beneficial for teeth and the feet.

Black Tourmaline – Black Tourmaline can be used to both repel and protect against negativity. It enhances physical well-being by increasing vitality, emotional stability and insight. It's said to give the user compassion and the ability to help see another's point of view. Worn on the body, tourmaline is thought to prevent cholesterol coagulation and build-up in blood vessels. It's also thought to purify the blood and promote sound sleep.

Obsidian – This is a very powerful stone and has always been associated with guardian spirits that watch over us. It is connected to protection on many levels. Obsidian in general helps to alleviate pain by reducing tension and releasing energy. It's also said to accelerate the physical healing of wounds. Obsidian is an excellent stone simply to have around, used to absorb and transform the negative energies into positive energy. It will vibrate calmness and security and also stabilize the energies of all persons within its reach. By grounding spiritual energy in the physical plane, obsidian connects both the mind and emotions. It absorbs and destroys negative energies, clearing any subconscious blockages you may have, then releases your stresses.

Hematite – This stone strengthens our connection with the Earth, making it an excellent grounding stone that leaves you feeling safe and fully alert. It endows us with courage, strength, endurance and vitality. Hematite stimulates concentration and enhances memory and inspiration. It absorbs negative energy and prevents you from taking on the negativity of others. Hematite is strong and is good for boosting self-esteem, enhancing willpower and imparting confidence. Hematite is used in healing blood conditions, such as anaemia and is also said to aid the treatment of leg cramps, anxiety and insomnia, according to archaeologists who found evidence of cocoa deposits in a ceramic pot near Guatemala.

Drunk on occasion by most people, cocoa used to be a more regular beverage of the more privileged. This included priests, rulers, soldiers and other members of a high social rank hundreds of years ago. They would ferment then roast the cocoa beans, grind them into a paste and mix into a drink. They would then add spices such as chillies, ginger, or vanilla. Sugar, however, was not available, so the cocoa paste was turned into a frothy drink, which they then consumed unsweetened. It was said that a drink of cocoa would leave you feeling extremely refreshed and could also sustain a person, without the need of food, for a whole day. Centuries ago it was often given to soldiers who were going into battle, such were its qualities.

Shamans would also use part of the cocoa bean for grounding themselves whilst undertaking spiritual ceremonies. They have continued using the cocoa bean for such purposes for centuries. A shaman is a person who works together with both the normal world and the spirit world as a medium. They are common in many tribal cultures. Shamanism may also exist in other types of culture throughout the world. Shamans would sometimes mix the cocoa paste into foods, as well as drinks, for medicinal, spiritual or ceremonial purposes.

Nowadays we find that cocoa is mixed with sugar and milk fats to produce a much sweeter product, but the benefits are still the same. One American chap, Chris Kilham, said about chocolate: "After water, cocoa is the single healthiest substance you can put in your mouth. It can easily replace a number of psychiatric drugs for mood, plus it produces the same chemistry in the brain that occurs when we fall in love." Chris Kilham lectures extensively on holistic health and botanical medicines throughout the United States. He also lectures in the European Union, Hong Kong, Thailand, Dubai, Australia, Peru, Vanuatu and many other countries. He is known in the U.S. as TV's FOX news medicine hunter and is also an author. Look him up if you are interested as he has a huge amount of information regarding health and natural medicine. His work is simply fascinating and he also shares my love of chocolate.

So the bottom line is that chocolate works rather well as a grounding method. So have a nibble when you want to ground yourself, preferably a darker, purer chocolate with a high percentage of cocoa solids. That does not mean a whole box, even if it's for a good reason! Just a small bar is fine and besides, it's a small taste of heaven.

"Keep close to nature's heart...

and break clear away, once in a while,

and climb a mountain or spend a week in the woods.

Wash your spirit clean."

John Muir

Chapter 9: With Great Power Comes Great Responsibility

'With Great Power Comes Great Responsibility', was one of my favourite lines from the first Spiderman film, with Toby MacGuire as Spidey himself. It was at an early point in the first film, when Uncle Ben is talking to Peter (Spiderman). Uncle Ben utters the words of wisdom before Spidey gets his outfit made up and swings around New York cleaning up the streets. What I am trying to say here is that you may have the best intentions in the world, but what you are doing can affect the lives of people you come into contact with, quite dramatically at times, so tread cautiously. Although I have tried to keep this book quite humorous and light (honestly this is the light version!), you do have to question your motives for what you are doing. Curiosity is great and clairvoyance can be fun, BUT take into account that people who are bereaved are often extremely vulnerable. They are open to abuse from those whose intentions are not good. Some people will hang on to your every word because they are desperate for some form of comfort. Others will not even entertain the idea of speaking to you and won't listen to anything you have to say. Even if *you* strongly believe that a spirit wants to make contact with them, or that you can help them, you cannot force someone to listen.

Grief takes many forms; knowing how to handle someone who is grieving is an incredibly responsible job in itself, let alone passing on messages from a person they knew who has died. I have had training on counselling and know how to advise a person on the best way to cope with certain issues. This is a huge part of being a medium, as many people come to you because they are bereaved or unhappy. It's therefore not appropriate to push your clairvoyant skills on to people when they have not asked for it. Neither is it appropriate to deliver messages in places that are not suitable to have a conversation, even if 'Mum or Dad' is very keen to talk. I had a situation like this once when I was shopping. A lady on the checkout started talking to me and, at just about the same time, her Mum decided to come through in spirit. The lady was telling me how she was not looking forward to Christmas that year because her Mum had recently died and she missed her terribly. She said how her Mum had made Christmas special for the whole family and spent much time in the kitchen. Her Mum had loved Christmas, but now she had gone Christmas felt awful. The lady then got quite emotional and had to stop herself from crying. Now I knew that Mum was right next to her and also connected to me. The connection was so strong that I had to hold my head because I felt like my hair was about a foot above my head. My spiritual aerial was going crazy and I knew without doubt that 'Mum' wanted to tell her that she was fine and was very much with her in spirit. The problem was that her daughter was on a checkout at work. It was not appropriate for me to casually say: 'By the way, Mum's fine and sends lots of love, she says she's actually with you a lot in spirit'. The poor woman would have either been an emotional wreck, or would have told me to 'bog off'. She may not have even believed me. It was not appropriate for me to spend time with her trying to convince her that Mum was actually with me. She had not asked for this situation or for any form of comfort, so I didn't say anything other than the fact that she must find it very difficult. I drove home an emotional wreck straight after. It was awful, as I was feeling Mum's anguish. As soon as I got home, I was almost in floods of tears myself, which is not something I tend to do after shopping, no matter how bad the queues are at Christmas!

I am not going to preach to you about <u>how</u> you should develop your clairvoyance. The following may be a little controversial to those mediums that have learned their skills by keeping to a strict procedure. Many mediums probably would not approve of what I am writing here, but I don't think that you always need to follow certain procedures. There are several I have come across, such as: not eating for several hours before meditating, never smoking or drinking alcohol, eating only healthy or pure foods and meditating quietly for at least an hour before even attempting to communicate with spirit. I am not suggesting for a millisecond that this is wrong, it's not, but you can still communicate with spirit without such a strict regime. Just have common sense, good intentions and be respectful. If you do communicate with spirit, make sure it's in an appropriate place. Once people know you have the 'ability', you may find yourself getting asked for readings fairly frequently. Down the pub or local watering hole on a Friday night may be one of those places. I would advise that you avoid doing readings in such a public place. You wouldn't ask a hairdresser for a quick cut if you saw them at the bar, would you? And hopefully, you would not want your counsellor or psychiatrist giving you advice in the pub, particularly if they had drunk a lot of alcohol. So try not to be tempted to do the same thing, as alcohol will cloud your judgement. In the same way that I do not drink alcohol before giving a reading, I will not give a reading to someone who is clearly drunk, either. The messages are fuzzy and your reading will not be as clear as when both of you are totally sober, trust me on this one. I personally think it's also disrespectful to communicate to spirit if under the influence of drink or drugs, and although tempting, I just find it wrong. If I were in spirit I would not appreciate trying to communicate through a drunken medium; messages are difficult enough at times to interpret, let alone with the added complication of alcohol or drugs. In fact, to be fair, talking to living people who are drunk can be a complete nightmare, so please take this into account. It may seem like a great idea at the time, but you may come to regret it later.

In the same way that you would show respect at someone's funeral, and you wouldn't say something inappropriate, the same applies when reading for someone. Be careful of what you say, even if the message you are getting is quite clear. Just because the message is from a spirit, it does not mean it has to be spoken. So if Grandma says something like, 'Your husband is still completely useless and you should get a divorce', be diplomatic! Put the message a different way, rather than coming straight out with it. Instead you could say: 'Grandma mentions that it looks like you're struggling with some issues within your marriage. These need to be addressed, or it may end up in divorce'. Never tell anyone what to do, particularly if the message is a sensitive subject, even if 'Mum, Dad, brother and sister' all come through in spirit and say the same thing. It's for the individual to choose how to live their life and not anyone else's decision, living or otherwise. If the message is something like 'You are far too bogged down with work and home, you need to make time for yourself', then this is fine; positive messages are always great. Everyone who visits you for a reading should always leave feeling much better than when they first came in. Remember that a relative in spirit will be the same as when they were alive. Just because they are dead, it doesn't mean that their advice will be perfect. If their advice was dodgy when alive, being in spirit is not going to make the blindest bit of difference.

The clearest readings you will have will be for those people who are open; those you can identify with personally and when you are working in a quiet, private environment. For example, I find I can easily read for those who have lost a parent or adult or those who have shared similar life experiences as me. The information just flows. When you have experienced the same form of bereavement, or experience and want to comfort those who are experiencing it too, your reading will also flow; it will almost seem effortless. If you take into account the points listed below, you will find your readings are much clearer and accurate.

- Being clean helps, it leaves you feeling more spiritual. It may sound mad but it's true!
- Read for those who have asked you to read for them, or for those who you know would be receptive; if you are not sure, don't do it.
- Go somewhere private, or find an environment that is conducive to clairvoyance.
- Try to calm the mind, or meditate, for about 10minutes before a reading.
- Make sure you are feeling well and rested in yourself. If you are

unwell, or have 101 things on your mind, or just had a blazing row with someone, then you are not going to be able to focus.

- Do not drink alcohol; make sure the person you are reading for has not drunk any alcohol either. Drugs are out, too, I am afraid, as the connection becomes fuzzy.

- Have good intentions. A person should always leave you feeling happy, knowing that their loved ones are with them.

- End on a positive note and thank the spirit involved for talking to you. Thank your guide, too.

- Always give 100% of the reading. I often found that I held back around 5% or 10% of the information, because I was either unsure or thought that the information wasn't relevant. It was often that particular 5% that was the most important.

- Be prepared to get it wrong. It may be our interpretation that is wrong or that the connection is fuzzy, like getting interference on a radio. Names may be misheard, so I tend not to give names unless very clear. If you decide to give a name and get it wrong, don't worry, you are learning.

- Remember that this is a gift. If you take it for granted or become a little too arrogant about it, it can be easily taken away again. You may find yourself giving the most awful reading ever; this will be in order to get your feet back on the ground. Trust me, it will knock your confidence and put you back in your place. One lady I know decided to announce to the world that she was a medium and had the word 'clairvoyant' and her phone number plastered all over her car. After a few weeks she was giving the most terrible readings and her reputation was rapidly ruined. This was all because she was far too concerned with making money and with the kudos attached to being classed as a 'professional' medium.

- Do not be tempted to try reading for a close friend or family member, even if you both feel like you want to, particularly when you are learning. It's very difficult to ascertain if the information you get is something that you have delved into the recesses of your mind to grasp, or if you really have made a connection. You will probably find that you may end up doing more harm than good; not necessarily to the friend or family member you are with, but to your own confidence or self-belief.

I tried to read for my Mum some time ago and, although it seemed to work, I very much regretted it later. My Grandmother on my mother's side never got to know her own mother who had to give her up at the age of 2-3years in the 1920s. My Mum had searched records and had some details which showed that my Great- Grandmother and her sisters had all died and there were no living relatives who could fill in the gaps for us. My Mum asked if I could connect clairvoyantly to see if I could find out what had happened, so as a fledgling medium I wanted to 'prove' to her that I was not totally bonkers. I did not know any information, other than the fact that my Grandmother never knew her own mother and that was all I had been told. I decided to give it a go and the information seemed to come through quite well; it was not a great connection, but it was a connection. Mum sat there with pen in hand jotting down notes, as I went through my chatter and did my thing. She then went off later and did some further research, taking into account the information I had given her. Now the main message I was getting clearer than any other information, was that Great Grandma had never forgotten her beautiful daughter and had much love for her. She was sorry she had to give her up but felt that she had no choice in this matter. She was telling me 'I had no choice, I had to go'. All of the information I did get could not be verified or proven by anyone, as no-one knew exactly what happened so I would never know if I was right or not, or if I had misinterpreted any of it. This was immensely frustrating for me as some things I had 'seen' very clearly and I wanted to check if I was right. I saw quite clearly my Great Grandma in hospital being shouted at by the matron. Two people were holding her back whilst the matron shouted at her, 'Elsie May, put that baby down right now, he is not yours anymore!' I could see my Great Grandma being very upset and tearful and shouting back at the matron. My mother told me afterwards that this baby was my Grandmother's brother, who was raised by his Grandma; in other words my Great Grandma's mother- in - law. So I knew she had left a baby. That bit was accurate.

The information I was getting clearly was not the information that my mother was looking for; she wanted facts, dates, place names, a new husband's name, all of which I was getting bits of, but nothing that clear. When Mum called me a few days later, to say that she had finally found Great Grandma records, she said that they were under a new married name. Mum was sending off for her death certificate and was thrilled. None of the information I had given her ended up leading to this finding so she was also questioning some of my information. She had drawn her own conclusions using the evidence she had found. It turns out that Elsie (Great Grandma) had registered the birth of her son, which my mother had discovered when she looked at the son's birth certificate, but Elsie had left him and her other family a few weeks later. Her marriage had been loveless and abusive; Elsie had wanted to leave for some time, but found herself pregnant with her son. Although her mother- in law- took care of both children begrudgingly when Elsie left, her husband had nothing to do with her during those 2 weeks she stayed with the family. He re-married soon after Elsie left and was not a good father to his children. We have no idea about what happened to Elsie after that for many years, but we know that she re-married in Birmingham some 22 years later. This then begs the question, why was I seeing Elsie being shouted at by the matron, who said that the 'baby was not hers to keep', if Elsie then registered his birth a few weeks later? Was my information wrong? I felt that it was quite clear, but I could not explain why it appeared to be wrong. Some of my information was spot on, but the rest could not be proven, so we will never know what really happened either way. My mother felt I was wrong in some of my reading and I felt that she doubted my new 'ability', which at the time totally shattered my confidence. After this I vowed never read for a family member again. She's fine with me now, but at the time when I was starting out it was incredibly frustrating. This is something else to bear in mind. If a person does not know much about the person who has passed and cannot validate much, then it may be better to not give a reading. It is wonderful when you receive that validation and very frustrating when you don't. So check before a reading to ascertain if a person knows enough about the spirit you're connected to.

In the beginning, when I began trying to make contact with spirit, I would only hear messages at night before I went to sleep and on waking in the morning. It was when I was just in between states of waking and sleep where I could choose to go either way. I was not awake enough to plan my day and be fully alert. I would still be a little sleepy, but not so sleepy that I would go straight back to sleep. Some people refer to this as being 'half asleep', when you are not quite in either state. This was my best time for messages as I was in a state of total relaxation and you may find you are the same.

You may also find that you readily acquire some messages or feelings when you are with someone. You may find that you have the feeling that they have lost a loved one, or that you can sense someone with them. Reading messages for someone is quite patchy in the early days. You may only get a few bits of information, or find that the information you do get may be difficult to interpret, so to reiterate, 'Say it and sod it'. If you get it wrong then you do; there are certain things you can do to help make a good connection, which have been mentioned above.

Working with someone you don't know is a good way to check if your information is accurate. An easy way to do this is to either join a clairvoyant group, spiritual church or an internet group, in which you can practise your skills, if you have no-one to practise with. Try getting a recommendation from someone before joining a group; this helps to check if the group is what you are looking for and that it is teaching at a level you are comfortable with. If it is an internet group, it will not matter if a person is communicating with you over the internet, as spirit can be with us at anytime, anywhere. As long as you can practise and develop at a suitable pace, you should do well. It does help to have a response from someone, purely to tell if your information is accurate or not, so you can learn.

When reading for someone, try not to ask questions, but use statements to which the other person can answer 'Yes, No or Don't Know 'instead and then only get them to elaborate if you need something clarified. If they give you too much information, it's easy to think that your logical mind has stepped in and made certain connections. If you are using simple statements such as, 'I feel you had a very happy childhood' or, 'I sense that you have lost you mother', it can be easier than 'Did you have an unhappy childhood?' or, 'Who is the woman is spirit?' By asking an open question you are instigating a conversation and the person you are reading for may give you more information than you need. You will get a much more positive result if you are given very few facts, as then you will know it's your clairvoyant skills that have given you the information, rather than using guesswork.

Exercise 9 – Is There Anybody There?

Before trying to read for someone or contacting spirit, it's a very good idea to quieten your own mind first. For those of you who can meditate, try using the following exercise as this one works particularly well for clairvoyance. For those who struggle with meditation, try the Pranic breathing exercise mentioned before.

Start by finding somewhere quiet first of all, as you do not want to be disturbed for 10 minutes or so. As in earlier exercises, put relaxing meditation music on if it helps and sit comfortably upright, or lay down straight if you prefer. If you are sitting in a chair, make sure your feet are on the ground, legs uncrossed and that you have a straight back. The energy needs to be able to flow through you.

Begin by concentrating on your breathing. Breathe in deeply through your nose and exhale fully. This can be back through the nose, or through the mouth, then close your eyes. Lay your hands on your lap, in an open position, then concentrate on your breathing. Imagine a bright, white light coming out from your abdomen and surrounding you in a large, white glow.

Now picture yourself sitting down on a bench in a small garden. It's a warm day and you are barefoot. You are wearing light, comfortable clothes and you are feeling particularly relaxed and happy. The garden is full of fragrant flowers and shrubs, which you can clearly smell in the air. There are climbing sweet peas and honeysuckle around the walls of the garden, together with lots of bright and beautiful flowers all around you. Notice the colours and fragrances of the flowers as you get up to walk through the garden, along a small path. You can feel the sun warm above you and hear the sounds of the birds in the trees.

Beyond the garden walls is a beautiful wooded area with rustling trees and wild flowers. You notice a small wooden gate at the edge of the garden that leads out to the wooded area. You walk out through the gate and along a new path, into the woods. You can feel the grass beneath your feet and smell the pine of the trees. It's a very lush and green wood, with tall trees around you. This makes you feel calm and safe. You see in front of you a large tree with an opening in its trunk. You walk through the opening in the tree, into a large hollow with five doors. Choose one of these doors to go through.

As you walk through the door, you enter a small round room and see a monk inside who has been waiting for you. Picture this monk, what does he look like? What is he wearing? He is standing behind a table, which has a silver goblet placed on it and lots of small, beautiful coloured glass bottles. All of the bottles contain a liquid; these have magical qualities to help you heighten your senses. Choose one of the bottles and ask the monk if you may drink what is in the bottle. He will smile and say, 'Of course you can, the contents will make you feel calm and safe, and enhance your senses'. He pours the liquid out from the bottle and into the goblet. He hands the goblet to you. You notice the colour of the liquid and then drink the contents. The monk invites you to sit for a moment in a large comfortable chair whilst you feel the effects of the drink. You feel incredibly peaceful and yet refreshed. Sit for a minute or so and enjoy the sensations you have.

It's now time to leave and you thank the monk for the drink he has given you. This has left you feeling wonderfully sensitive and peaceful. You walk back through the door, out of the tree trunk and into the woods again, feeling the grass back underneath your feet. You hear the birds chirping and smell the pine and bracken around you. The garden is just in the distance, so you walk back through the trees, until you arrive back at the gate. Open the gate and walk through the garden. You soon arrive at the bench where you first began. When you are ready, start to feel the surroundings in the room you are in, then slowly open your eyes.

You are now ready to make contact with spirit and work with your guide. Most mediums can sense when their guide is present and working with them, which is often felt through a subtle physical sensation. As I said before, I get a tingling sensation at the front of my head when I sense my guide. Others have felt a subtle touch on the arm or shoulder when their guide is present, a little like a feather has stroked them. Notice what you feel when you connect to your guide. Don't worry if you do not feel anything to begin with as it tends to become more noticeable over time.

Now, can you sense a person around you? Again you may get a physical sensation, or just a feeling. I start with the feeling of someone in the vicinity and then the contact becomes stronger. It then turns into a tingling sensation in the back of my head once I start talking to them.

Go through the following points and see what information you sense. Remember you should ask a spirit questions, such as:

Is this person a male or female?

Approximately how old are they?

Is this a tall person or short person; if you were to stand up where would they be in comparison to you?

Are they a large build, average or petite?

How do they make you feel, what sort of emotions are you getting?

Do you get the feeling of a relationship to someone such as a parent, grandparent, brother or sister or child?

If the connection starts to become weaker, or you find yourself momentarily stuck, see if you can identify a significant month. This will usually be a birthday, anniversary or month of death.

Ask how they died. You may be given the sensation of how they died. For example, you may find yourself having breathing difficulties, or you may feel an ache or pain in part of your body. Trust these sensations, as they are usually significant.

Ask if there are other family members, living or passed.

Ask if there is a message for the person you are reading for.

Be observant of your own body language, as this is often linked to spirit.

When you have finished communicating, which I would recommend to do for a maximum of an hour, you will need to do something to ground yourself. This is where you bring yourself fully back to Earth and connect with reality again. You can do this by either going outside for a while, or by putting your feet on the ground, picturing roots coming out from your feet and growing into the ground. Imagine all of your clairvoyant energy pouring out of you and into the ground. There are other methods too and these, are covered in a lot more detail in exercise 8.

Guidance Tips

If when you try this nothing much comes through, do not worry. Sometimes it takes a little while to get clear messages and sometimes spirit simply does not come though very clearly at all. When I started, I found that initially I would receive very little information. Others in our development circle would have reams of information, which left me quite envious and feeling a bit anxious. They would start by saying, 'I can see a man or woman standing behind ...' (this would be someone in our development circle). They would get names, dates, emotions, long messages, and could also tell how the person had died. I would find myself staring at the space behind the person and not see anything at all! No matter how badly I wanted to, I just could not see what they were seeing. Over the weeks this began to change quite dramatically, just by practising and I would get the sensation of a man or a woman being next to someone in our circle. When I relaxed more, but focused (I know it sounds odd), I would feel the relationship such as a grandmother or father and the information began to filter through.

The key thing here is to ASK, ASK and ASK!!! Many times I would get a feeling of someone and would then think, 'who is this person?', as I was not getting a clear connection and Jody would say to me 'how tall do you think they are?', and I found I would know. She then prompted me with questions such as 'how do they make you feel?', and I found I had the answers. So even though I felt like I was *not* getting a lot of information coming through, when it came down to it, I was! The other thing to take into account is that the information usually starts off gently and then flows after a minute or two. If you are with a person, just begin talking and telling them what you are sensing or feeling from the spirit you are connected to. It may start slowly but they will be able to confirm your information, or steer you back on track. Once you start talking the information keeps coming. I have no idea why this is the case but it just seems to work. So start by saying if you sense a male or female, give their height, their build and age if possible. If you find you begin to dry up, try focusing on how the spirit makes you feel and this will help you to refocus. I find that when I concentrate, I can get a good idea of the sort of person they were. For example, some people make me feel warm and loved and others make me feel a bit wary of them. Spirits work in the same way. Some feel like they would have been quite feisty when alive, or a bit of a lovable rogue, whilst others are very quiet and gentle. You will find most spirits are more than willing to talk to you if you ask them something. They won't always give the information straightaway; so sometimes you *will* need to ask them for it.

Jody went through a very quick exercise with us in our group. It was a simple yet brilliant way of explaining how difficult it can be for a medium to get information, if they don't ask for it. She took two of us from our group and asked me to be the spirit daughter of the other lady, with herself acting as the medium. The conversation went like this:

'Amy, you've died of a heart attack and Emma is your Mum. I will act as the medium for you, what message do you want to give to your Mum?'

Me: *'Tell her that I know she misses me but I am absolutely fine and send lots of love.'*

Medium: *'Emma, I have a lady with me who knows you miss her, but she says she is fine and sends lots of love.'*

Emma: *'That's great, but who is this lady? I have a few ladies I know in spirit.'*

You can see by this brief exercise that *I know* that Emma is my Mum, but she has no idea that I am her daughter. This is why, as a medium, you have to ask. Spirit does not automatically come with huge amounts of information, it's as though they expect you as the medium to know who *they* are. Remember that you are the middle person passing the message, so spirit is only aware that they have made a connection and will pass on the messages that *they* want to pass on. What you have to do as a medium is ask the questions in order to identify them, then use all of your senses to gather information. So the conversation would be better like this:

Medium: *'Okay I have a lady with me who feels about 40years old.'*

Medium to Me: *'Who are you to Emma and what message do you want to give to her?'*

Me to Medium: *'I am her daughter, Amy. Tell her that I know she misses me, but I am absolutely fine and send my love.'*

Medium to Emma: *'She says she is your daughter Amy and knows you miss her, but she says she is fine and sends her love'*

Emma to Medium: *'That is wonderful, I do miss her. Can you tell me anything else?'*

Medium to Me: *'How did you pass, Amy and do you have any brothers or sisters?'*

Me to Medium: *'I have no brothers or sisters; I am the only child'.* Now I may tell the medium that I had a heart attack, or I may give them the sensation of a pain in their chest, which is more common. It won't be as if the medium is having a full blown heart attack. It will be much more subtle and they may experience a little discomfort.

Medium to Emma: *'She is saying she was the only child and I am getting the sensation of a shortness of breath and a pain in my chest; it feels very tight.'*

Emma to Medium: *'Amy died of a heart attack, so I imagine that is what you are feeling.'*

This should give you an idea of how information comes through and the questions you need to ask. If you do not ask or pry, you are unlikely to receive much information and you want to be able give clear and accurate readings. Any person can say, 'I have Grandma here and she sends her love', which may well be the case, but you should be able to do better than that. Spirit will want their loved ones to know they are okay and still with them, so 99% of the time they will be forthcoming with information. You do have to take into account there may be some subjects that are difficult for them to speak about or broach, so please do not worry if at times it's difficult to acquire certain pieces of information. If a subject was difficult for spirit to talk about when they were alive, then it's probably still difficult to discuss even though they have passed on.

Be aware of your body language and sensations! I was so quick to dismiss my own body language as feelings of awkwardness or being fidgety that I was missing huge chunks of information. You will find that if you stand up when you connect to spirit, you will get a better connection and you want to be more aware of your body language. You will begin to do things naturally that are connected to spirit without even realising it. I found myself twiddling with a ring on various occasions without noticing or even thinking about it. Jody pointed this out to me and asked what this could mean. I told her that I guessed it could mean that the person I was reading for had a ring belonging to the spirit I was connected to. Then, when I asked the recipient, they had. This has never been wrong for me yet and every time I start to twiddle with a particular silver ring I know that the person I am reading for also has a ring that is connected to the spirit. I also find that if I was standing up I would start to hold or rub parts of my body, such as my stomach, shoulders, or head. I have since found that this is connected to how the spirit has died. My readings are so much better when standing; the energy just flows. The area I am holding or rubbing does not necessarily hurt at all, I just find myself holding or rubbing those areas as I am talking. I am doing it completely without thinking about it. The other thing I find I do is to rub the top of my lip with my fingertips from both hands. Or I rub my chin with my hand. I never noticed either of these things before it was pointed out to me and just thought I was trying to overcome my awkwardness at being upright. In fact it was an indicator that the spirit was a man with a moustache or beard when alive. It really is so subtle, but very clever!

At a BBQ I went to recently, my friend who is currently going through a messy divorce, talked about her new boyfriend she has been with for the last few months. The whole time she was talking I was twirling my engagement and wedding rings. Four or more years ago I wouldn't have thought anything of it at all; I always thought that I was a bit of a twiddler right back to my school years with either rings or bracelets, etc. Now I know that it screams out a message. I know beyond doubt that an engagement is on the cards for my friend. I am 100% sure, because I have learnt that when my guide makes me twiddle my wedding ring, he is communicating a message. It's not me doing it randomly, it's his way of talking to me.

If you are still struggling, go through the bullet points mentioned earlier in this chapter and see if there is anything you can do to help the connection. Check if there is something you haven't asked the spirit that maybe you should be aware of. If you have a lot on your mind, or have been unwell, your connection will not be as clear as if you are feeling fabulous and calm. Also remember that this is a different language that you are using. If it were sign language, for example, and you got something wrong, you would probably laugh it off and not think about it. This is harder because you are more than likely terrified of making an idiot out of yourself. The more you let go of this fear, the easier your connection will be.

"Knowledge is proud that it knows so much;

Wisdom is humble that it knows no more."

William Cowper

Chapter 10: Chakras

You may recall that I talked about chakras earlier on in the book, now I will do my best to simply explain what these are. I will also describe where they are placed and what they do.

All of us have seven main chakras (literally translated as wheels) placed within our body which act as energy centres or batteries. Our chakras radiate energy outwards and also draw energy inwards from our surrounding environment. Each chakra is responsible for governing different physical and emotional aspects in us – physically through the organs or glands in our body, and emotionally through our mental and spiritual states. They all work in harmony for the benefit of the whole person, but chakras can become unbalanced. If we are in an unhealthy environment where our home life and working life are unhappy, we will literally absorb that negative energy in through our chakras. When part of a chakra is unbalanced, it can end up affecting us on a mental or physical level. An out of balance chakra is usually caused by being over-active, under-active, or blocked. These are definitely worth researching and making a note of if you are interested in methods of healing, such as Reiki. This is because a lot of spiritual healing is based on unblocking chakras. However, you only need to focus on three of the chakras in particular for the purpose of clairvoyance.

Blockages can be caused through all sorts of unhealthy activity, such as the food we eat, the people we associate with, the environment we live in and our emotional state of mind. Basically, blockages are caused by doing anything that is impure or negative, which sounds a little dull, to be honest! Now I am not going to say that you all have to live perfectly healthy lives, in which you eat like a poor Japanese fisherman, meditate daily, avoid alcohol at all costs and never have a negative thought. If we all lived like this there would be no point in living at all and I for one would last only a day at the very most. So with that in mind, I will describe to you the chakras that work for the use of clairvoyance and how to keep them whirring away quite merrily. Each chakra is associated with a colour and is numbered one to seven, starting at the groin and ending at the crown of your head.

1. The Root Chakra is our life- force energy. It's also called our Red or Base Centre
2. The Spleen Chakra is our sensing and feeling energy. It's also called our Orange or Splenic Centre
3. The Solar Plexus Chakra is our mental energy. It's also called our Yellow or Ego Centre
4. The Heart Chakra is our emotional energy. It's also called our Green or Cardiac Centre
5. The Throat Chakra is our communication energy. It's also called our Blue or Laryngeal Centre
6. The Brow Chakra is our intuitive energy. It's also called our Indigo or Third-Eye Centre
7. The Crown Chakra is our inspiration and spiritual energy. It's also called our Violet or Coronal Centre.

We will be focusing on numbers three, - the solar plexus in the stomach, six - the brow above the eyes and seven - the crown on top of the head. I am going to try keeping this extremely simple so you don't get bogged down with too much detail. Quite honestly, if you try to remember and perform every little detail that you are supposed to, before contacting spirit, you will end up starting at 5.00am for an evening reading.

The third chakra in our solar plexus, placed just above the navel, gives us our self-confidence, humour and the ability to think rationally. It's where your 'gut instinct' originates from and it can be very helpful when performing a reading. If, for example, you have received some information from spirit which feels right, but the person you are reading for is looking at you blankly or says 'no', then try looking at it from a different angle and it will probably be right. I had an instance once where I was describing a woman, who had passed over, to her daughter. I knew without a doubt that it was the woman's mother that I was connected to and I described her as 'quite a large lady', to which the daughter said 'no'. I checked again, and was quite definite that she was not a slim or petite lady, but the daughter was quite adamant I was wrong. I talked about this with Jody afterwards, as I was so convinced that I was right. It turned out that Jody knew the daughter and had brought her mother through herself. Jody told me how the mother was about a size 18, but then became much thinner due to cancer. Had I have stuck with this information, or asked if she had lost weight due to her cancer, then the daughter may have said 'yes', but in this instance she didn't. Despite my gut instinct telling me I was right, I dismissed my information and moved on. Should this happen to you, try sticking with what you feel. Your third chakra will be whirring away trying to tell you that you are right and it will do the same similarly, when something is wrong. The trick here is to recognise it - and stick to your guns!

The sixth chakra is placed right in the middle of your forehead and is referred to as the 'Third Eye', or brow chakra. This gives us our psychic ability and insight. A little like the third chakra, the sixth one also gives us intuition, but rather than coming from the gut, it comes from your head. This is where you will find yourself knowing information without being able to explain why. Sometimes you may see or sense things which are completely correct, a little like when you know that 'something' is wrong. When this happens, it will be your brow chakra that is spinning away happily.

The seventh chakra is your crown chakra and is found right on the very top of your head. This chakra gives us our spiritual drive and our need to learn about a higher intelligence. We use this one when we connect our energy with that of spirit or higher beings, a little like a merging of minds. Quite often we will get sparks of inspiration and wisdom, which occur when this chakra is fully open and spinning as it should. Those 'Eureka' moments will be down to this wheel. When this chakra is running smoothly, it will feel as if we are being naturally guided and inspiration will feel almost effortless. Those writers and creative people who find themselves suddenly lacking in inspiration, or faced with writers' block, may find that this little wheel has become a bit clogged or imbalanced.

Each chakra, when unbalanced, can create a host of symptoms in a person, such as headaches, stomach complaints and blood disorders. To be honest, having researched this, every single ache pain and ailment can be attributed to a blocked or imbalanced chakra. This may well be the case. If this is something that interests you, then there is just as much information available, as there are ailments. There are also an abundance of books and reading literature available. A good Reiki, or spiritual healer, can help with these symptoms should you be experiencing them. Many healers have said that even if you don't believe that healing will work, or have doubts about how it works, it's still very effective. I have never visited one myself, but have met several healers who have had fantastic results. So like with most spiritual things, I would say if you feel this is for you, give it a go. I am going to go through some things to try to keep your three chakras spinning effectively that are concerned with clairvoyance only.

Exercise 10 – Spinning Wheels

The Third Chakra - To keep your third chakra in good working order, keep your mind active by doing anything that involves using some brain power. Crosswords, puzzles and reading any informative material should also help. As the third chakra is associated with yellow, then apparently yellow foods also help. As this chakra is concerned with digestion, you could try oil of evening primrose as a supplement, which is also recommended for the cursed PMT. Some healers recommend using aromatherapy, so a massage using essential oils is recommended, or alternatively, use oil burners to flood your room with wonderful scents. Go for anything yellow, such as lemon, ginger, honeysuckle, and cinnamon (which is technically brown, but still okay). Also rosemary, which I know is green, but apparently it works with this chakra, too. Go out when the sun is shining, as you will be bathed in yellow 'feel good' light This will always make you feel calmer and happier. Yellow clothing and furnishings can also brighten your mood as well.

Yellow foods:

Yellow peppers

Sweet corn

Parsnips

Yellow tomatoes

Yellow lentils

Chickpeas

Cornflakes

Grapefruit

Pineapples

Melons

Bananas

Lemon

The Sixth Chakra - Moving on to your sixth chakra; to keep this wheel spinning happily, go outside to do a little cloud watching or stargazing; anything that involves looking up towards the heavens. Some spas have steam rooms or tepidariums (a warm room), with twinkling lights and crystals of predominantly purples and indigos. These are perfect for silencing the mind and getting some inspiration. Indigo oils, such as patchouli, frankincense, and jasmine, are said to be very beneficial, so fill your home with these scents. Do anything creative, such as writing, painting, or simply making something using your artistic skills. There are so many creative kits available, I am sure there will be something you can find that will get your creative juices flowing! Indigo coloured clothing or furnishings have also been said to help.

Foods for both the sixth and seventh chakras tend to be the same, so I have grouped them together and listed them below the seventh chakra information.

The Seventh Chakra – Your crown chakra is all about connecting with a higher being, or God. It's about finding time to talk our higher consciousness and letting go of the problems we face. This can be hard for some people, so do not struggle with it if you find this difficult. The other thing to try is to keep a dream journal. This, I think, can be quite fascinating, offering great insight into what our inner self is trying to say. Write down your aspirations and good intentions, so that you don't lose sight of them. Use lavender, violet, mulberry or wisteria oils for massage or oil burners. A lavender pillow can also help you sleep at night. Purple rooms are for great relaxing. I know of a purple room with padded walls that is used for calming children who have learning disabilities, when they are upset or frustrated. It sounds mad, but it's actually a great room. The temperature is slightly cooler than the standard 20°-25°C, and within 10-20 minutes most upsets with the children have been overcome; it works beautifully.

These foods are said to be filled with antioxidants and have huge benefits towards keeping healthy. I am afraid blue sweets do not count! The foods must be healthy and naturally coloured.

Indigo foods:

Blueberries

Blackcurrants

Grapes

Blackberries

Plums

Purple asparagus

Purple potatoes

Red cabbage

Aubergines

Purple kohlrabi

Purple broccoli

Raisins & Figs

The last exercise is to lie down flat, when you are nicely relaxed. Picture your chakras like CD's, hovering a few inches above your body. If you feel that one, or several chakras, are blocked, then imagine your 'CD' to be clogged up and turning slowly. If you are unsure how to tell which chakras are blocked, then imagine them all spinning very slowly. Visualize water, or oil, being slowly poured over the disc and gently cleaning it. This will be the same colour of the chakra. Then start to speed up this disc. If you are visualising all of your chakras, then it helps to remember that your chakras are coloured in the order of a rainbow, with red at the bottom and violet at the top, on your crown chakra. Picture the dirt washing off the disc, leaving it shiny and clean so that it's spinning quickly. Do this with each of your blocked chakras; it should only take a few minutes. If you can do this first thing in the morning before you get up, then you do not have to make a special effort and it should leave you set up for the day.

For clairvoyance, we predominantly need to open up our crown chakra. You can always try imagining this chakra as a large flower that opens up and shines out a bright, white light. Do this just before you communicate with spirit and then close it again when you have finished.

Guidance Tips

The above exercises are only suggestions and are not essential for clairvoyance to occur. They may help your clairvoyance by providing a better connection. Many mediums would swear by them. However, I truly believe that they are not a vital part. Do by all means try it, but if you struggle to visualise the exercise through meditation, then do not push yourself to continue.

There have been many times when I have given a perfectly accurate reading without going through all of the numerous rituals and rigmaroles before making contact with spirit. If we all had to go through every recommended ritual and obeyed every suggested rule to communicate with spirit, then how come we find spirits dropping in when shopping at the local supermarket, or when we least expect it? So if you decide not to do this before communicating with spirit, or forget to do it completely, please do not worry.

One experienced medium I knew, said she always had a bit of a problem herself with   chakras. She felt that sometimes she had accidentally closed her crown chakra, simply by the thought of it closing unintentionally. I remember a similar experience whilst in a development circle, where I imagined my crown chakra as a beautiful white lotus flower that had opened up. One moment it was there emitting a glorious white light, like a lighthouse attracting in spirits and the next I pictured it shut. I have no idea why, as I certainly didn't want it shut, but my imagination was not having any of it and my lotus flower was being opened and closed like a barn door. In the end, after becoming quite frustrated with myself, I threw the flower idea away and pictured just a white light coming out of the top of my head. This seemed to work exceptionally well for me, but not for others, so try both methods.

If you struggle in with any meditation or visualisation exercise, then never be afraid to adapt it so that it's easier for you to work with. I cannot stress enough that there is no right or wrong way to develop your clairvoyance, it really is a case of whatever works for you. All books and sources of information about spirituality are simply what someone *believes* to be true. It is not set in stone, just because it works for them. Many authors and writers talk of the same methods and processes, because they were taught the same way, or because a particular method works well for them, too. It does not guarantee that their methods will be right for you. Please use whatever works well for you in your circumstances. So if you find that basting yourself with blueberry juice, whilst singing 'The Rainbow Song' makes your clairvoyance more effective, then stick to that!

Chapter 11: Unwanted Guests and Exorcisms

I could not really write a book on spirituality without covering how to deal with unwanted spirits or house guests! As a medium you will possibly find yourself being called in to a house where the occupiers are in a bit of a state due to certain spiritual activity. As mentioned previously, this is rarely as exciting as it first seems. It is usually a bit of hysteria with the possible miffed spirit, or a psychic teenager who has a gift they are unaware of. Sometimes however, you do get the odd spirit who is distinctly more than a little miffed and is, instead, downright annoyed or unapproachable. This is very rare, but it does occur from time to time.

When practising your clairvoyant skills, you may find that you get the odd spirit in who does not feel particularly friendly, or comes across as a bit of a pain in the butt. When I previously read about 'low level entities' in spiritual books and how they could be aggressive, the thought of actually connecting with one scared me half to death. I certainly didn't want anybody taking over my body or getting inside my head. I had enough to deal with handling my own thoughts and day to day struggles! I certainly didn't want any other person's, living or otherwise, jumping in my head. So the first time it happened to me, I must admit I was surprised at how un-frightening it was. It was first thing in the morning and I was in bed. I was in that in-between state of waking and sleep, when I find myself most in-tune with the spirit world. I had various messages and thoughts popping into my head, then had another thought pop in which was not so friendly. The thoughts I had, were of someone swearing and calling me various colourful names. When I actually put it down into words it sounds quite awful and terrifying, but I can assure you it was not like that at all. The words dropped into my head exactly like a thought would. I didn't hear them out loud and I didn't feel like I was being possessed, not even remotely, it was just like a thought.

So as an example, imagine you see a homeless man on the street who shouts out an abusive remark. You probably wouldn't bat an eyelid, but would instead ignore it, or tell him politely to 'go away', if you get my drift. This felt exactly the same. I told him politely to 'go away' and that I was not interested, then pictured myself surrounded by a bubble of white light. It really was as simple as that and he went. It was not scary in any way at all, but more of a surprise if anything because I was not expecting it. So should you get similar thoughts pop into your head, or should you feel uncomfortable with a spirit, tell them to go away, then imagine a bubble of white light surrounding you. You are in control of what happens and you certainly do not have to put up with anything you are not happy with. If you picture yourself surrounded in white light before you begin connecting to spirit, then the chances are you won't receive any unwanted messages in the first place. As this happened to me early on in my development, I had not pictured the light around me to start with. This charming man had decided to make his presence known to me when I was not expecting it. I have only one had similar experience since then when I had not surrounded myself in light before connecting. Again it was someone who decided to say something completely mindless, so I sent them packing. It's no different than you would act towards a living person. If you treat them in the same way as you would someone living, then half of the fear has already gone. If you would not tolerate this from a stranger who is living, then you certainly don't have to tolerate it from anyone who happens to be otherwise.

Now for entities that are loitering in a house that need to be moved on, a similar method has to be applied. Treat them as you would a living person. If you had someone squatting in your house, I am sure you would not feel overly happy about it. After all, this is *your* house and they are most definitely unwelcome. Spirits are the same and need to be moved on. They need to be aware that they have died and are no longer welcome in your home.

Jody and I went to a house to speak to a gentleman and his son, about an unwanted guest or two that they had in residence. The gentleman, 'Peter', had described on the phone that his house was a hive of spiritual activity. His house had been built on crossed ley lines, which, according to Harper's Encyclopedia of Mystical and Paranormal Experience, are "alignments and patterns of powerful, invisible Earth energy said to connect various sacred sites, such as churches, temples, stone circles, megaliths, holy wells, burial sites and other locations of spiritual or magical importance. "

Peter said how the walls of his house were shaking; people were being pushed, ornaments were morphing into different shapes, and all in all there was a whole heap of activity that was scaring both him and his son. They were both sleeping downstairs because they were too afraid to go upstairs where most of the activity was happening. Peter had tried sage smudging to purify his house, but without success. Put simply, this is where a bunch of sage is set alight and then blown out so that the herbs continue to smolder. The resulting smoke is meant to cleanse the area concerned. Peter had also called in a group of people to perform an exorcism, which had only made things twice as bad and they were both at their wits' end. Both Jody and I were quite excited by the prospect of going to our first proper haunting together and we were bracing ourselves for a whole mass of spirit activity.

We arrived at a typical end- of -terrace house and were met by Peter, who was in his 50's, and his son 'Joe', who was 19years old. They invited us in and we sat down in their living room, whilst they explained what had been going on. A lot of activity had been happening around Joe, who had felt something nudging him physically and tugging at his clothes and bed sheets. Joe would also hear voices and could sense a huge wealth of information when touching objects owned by someone else. He was able to use psychometry very effectively, it would appear. Jody and I sat and talked to both Peter and Joe and explained how the spirit world was trying to get Joe's attention. Joe had a natural ability for clairvoyance, which had been becoming more apparent in the last year or so. Jody explained how this was very similar to her own experience and that Joe really needed to make a decision to accept his ability and learn how to control it, or block it out as much as possible using some methods that we could show him. As he had such an apparent natural ability, Jody told him that he would probably never fully be able to block spirit contact. He could instead make it manageable and possibly come back to it later, when and if he felt inclined to do so. It turned out that Peter also had some ability himself, but was struggling to keep himself grounded. He talked about spirits endlessly whist we were there, as if they were some fantastic phenomena that he *wanted* to be in contact with. He was actually encouraging the activity, in an odd way. He was scared of it because he didn't understand it, but was totally fascinated and wanted to talk about it with every person he met. Every time we talked to Joe about what was happening to him, Peter would cut in and describe the incident as a huge and terrifying event. Joe, on the other hand, was quite realistic about it recalling the events as being less dramatic. He, too, was afraid at times, but more than anything wanted to know why and how it happened. Dad, unfortunately, had hyped Joe up too much by constantly talking about the spiritual activity. He had convinced himself that he had a full- blown haunting with poltergeists. Both Jody and I checked with each other to see if either of us was sensing any spirits around us downstairs. We both agreed we weren't, so asked if we could check to see if there was something in his room. He asked if he could clear the bedroom a little before we went in as it was extremely cluttered and untidy. Once Peter had finished, we went upstairs.

We started in Joe's bedroom, which was an average teenage boy's room with nothing noticeably different. It was not particularly tidy and quite small, but nothing you wouldn't usually see. After a few minutes of sitting on his bed quietly, Jody asked me if I was sensing anything, to which I said 'no' as I was not sensing anything at all. It turned out that neither was she. We then did a brief meditation to see if a spirit wanted to say anything to us, or to pass on a message, and again we got nothing. Jody thought it would be a good idea to cleanse the room (spiritually!), just so that Joe would feel safe in his room and to remove any negative energy or feelings. Once this was completed we went into Peter's room. As soon as we went in, the energy of the room felt very different and extremely oppressive. There was clutter everywhere and it looked like the room hadn't been cleaned in a decade or more. There was an old black and white photograph of a well-dressed lady pinned up on the wall above the dado rail. It was at an angle and covered in thick dust. It was clearly Peter's Mum. As soon as we sat down on the bed, his mother came through very clearly - she was not a happy woman! She had been a very house- proud lady when alive and was quite horrified at the sorry state of her son's bedroom. To be pinned up on a wall gathering dust, looking over a room which looked appallingly neglected, was not her idea of being fondly remembered! Jody then told me that she could sense a man who had a long grey beard and hair. He was not overly happy either. This had been his house previously; he was most upset that the fireplace had been boarded up when he had not asked for it to be done. Jody then performed an exercise to take him towards the light, whilst I pictured Peter's mother being surrounded in a lovely pink light.

This seemed to do the trick and the room felt a lot lighter after we left; it didn't have such an oppressive feel. Once downstairs, we explained how both rooms had been cleansed and were now quite safe and spirit free. We told Peter how he really needed to clean his bedroom and make it a pleasant and relaxing place, for him as well as Mum. The message from Mum was delivered; Peter conceded that she had been extremely house- proud and he knew she would be upset to see it if still alive. He went on to say that he had suffered a long depression and illness, spending most time in his bedroom, which was why it was in its current state. When we explained the benefits of having a nice, clean room, he agreed that he needed to change it. Just like with meditation, a clean and clutter- free room is good for the soul;

it makes us instantly feel better and more inclined to want to spend time there. Both Peter and Joe needed to bring in some clean and positive energy to the house and to use their rooms as they normally would, by sleeping in them again.

It's very easy to hear every creak and bump in an old house and associate it with spiritual activity once you have experienced it, but after a cleansing has taken place you need to carry on as normal. Both Jody and I explained to Peter and Joe that they needed to treat spirits as living people, telling them to go if they are not wanted. This could be performed mentally, rather than verbally, and should still work. We described how people performing an actual exorcism, or similar, will nine times out of ten make matters worse. To give you an idea, imagine if the spirit was you and this was your house previously. You have new people in the house who can sense you, but are ignoring you. They then try to get rid of you by daubing holy water up the walls and chanting at you to make you leave. I am darned sure I would be pretty annoyed if it was me and would wonder why they had not just spoken to me in the first place. They would only need to ask why I was still there, or why I was troubled. The more they ignored me, the more I would get myself noticed. Talk to me like a living person and, if someone could communicate with me, then I would communicate back. It's not exactly rocket science.

After this we closed both Peter and Joe down to any activity that they were experiencing, then told them how to block any unwanted guests from dropping in. After Jody and I had finished, Joe and I spoke on our own about how he was feeling and I was able to answer some of his questions. He was quite aware of his abilities, just didn't understand why he had them or how to work with them. We chatted for about 15 minutes whilst Jody and Peter talked. Before leaving, we explained that each time they talked about any spiritual activity, they were almost opening the door to the spirit world again, so to keep any chat to a minimum. When we talk about spirits, we more or less send out a 'welcome sign' for them to drop in. If they have already made contact, you are unwittingly opening yourself up to spiritual activity without being aware of it. So in the instance of unwanted activity, the more we talk about spirits, the more they are likely to make an appearance, particularly if someone has a strong ability. Joe said that this was fine with him and that he would rather not bring up the subject. Peter, on the other hand, was already saying how he couldn't wait to tell his Thai wife what had happened with us and that he would call her later that day. We never heard back from either Peter or Joe, and as far as I know, everything has remained quieter. I had the feeling that they may get in touch again though. Peter was so fascinated by the subject of spirits, that it was almost consuming him. Hopefully, Joe would remember what we had told him about how to keep himself closed to spirits and what to do if one should happen to drop in.

Some houses, such as this one, have been built on ley lines which many people believe are magnets for spiritual activity. So in some cases it could be argued that these houses will always be a hive of activity, regardless of any spiritual 'cleansing'. The definition of ley lines, according to the Concise Oxford Dictionary states: Ley/Li/Lei: "The supposed straight line of a prehistoric track usually between hilltops".

It explained that birds, fish and other animals use ley lines almost as a 'Sat Nav' to direct them back to breeding grounds, or south to warmer climates in winter. Quite fascinating when you think about it!

The following article is about ley lines and spiritual activity, written by paranormal investigators Dave Wood, Anne Piper and Cindy Nunn for BBC Gloucestershire.

'The scientific belief, as previously explained, is that these lines are areas of altered magnetic fields. The more spiritual and romantic belief is that they ooze back the energy from all the people who have trodden these mystical, religious paths since time began. The general belief is that prehistoric man was aware of these cosmic lines under the Earth

120

and sought to build his sacred structures along them in order to tap into their magical properties. Major prehistoric structures of higher importance can frequently be found to occupy locations where two or more leys intersect with each other. The priests or shamans of prehistoric man would have been expected to find these leys and work out their connection with other existing monuments accordingly. It is also believed that many ancient groves, worshipped by the Druids, sit upon leys.

Generally it is believed that electro-magnetic fields can affect the body and mind. Other effects of this type of energy are said to be similar to those of static electricity: feelings of 'tingling' on the skin and hairs standing on end. The energy is thought to produce vibrations on a low frequency which, although inaudible to the human ear, can alter perception and create sensations of dizziness and unbalance. In extreme cases it is thought to be able to cause nausea and headaches. These symptoms mirror those often described by people who feel the presence of spirits.'

To me this makes perfect sense. If birds and other animals can pick up on the electromagnetic energy of the Earth, then mediums can also pick up on the same energies. Headaches, dizziness and nausea are the most common symptoms experienced by mediums; we actually feel the presence of spirits through their energy. If we work on another frequency, which we have to in order to be clairvoyant, then this will affect how we feel physically. Many people, who are not practicing mediums, often mention similar sensations when they have felt a presence of a spirit around them. Most comment about feeling a cold chill, or the hairs on the back of their neck standing up. This would be the energy of a spirit that they are picking up on.

I thought it may be interesting to note down some places that claim to be haunted, all of which have been built on sites where ley lines cross.

1. Wotton-under-Edge, Gloucestershire. The Ram Inn. The Ram claims to be the most haunted building in the country, with as many as 9 different entities haunting the pub. One of these is a lady called Elizabeth, who was apparently murdered in the pub and buried beneath the bar. The former inn dates back to the 12th century and was built on an ancient pagan burial site.

2. Woodchester Mansion, Stroud. This gothic-style Victorian mansion is said to be rife with ghosts. Several murders are said to have taken place at the mansion and it boasts a number of reported hauntings. The mansion was never completed after the original house, owned by William Leigh, was demolished. By the early 1870s construction workers and craftsmen who were in charge of re-building the mansion, mysteriously downed tools one day, never returning to reclaim them.

3. Prestbury, Cheltenham. This village on the outskirts of Cheltenham is allegedly the most haunted in England. Prestbury's streets are said to be haunted by the Black Abbot, a headless cavalier who was killed when a rope was stretched across a road; a ghostly knight, a medieval rider who was shot with an arrow, plus several spectral women.

4. Buckingham Palace, London. Buckingham Palace stands on the site of what was once a priory. The monk supposedly appears dressed in a chain bound brown habit on the rear terrace, and is only visible for a few minutes before he fades away. There are other spirits that have been seen, too, such as Major John Gwynne who shot himself at his desk on the first floor. He was the private secretary of Edward 7th and has been seen in what would have been his office.

5. Hampton Court, London. It has been claimed that Anne Boleyn has been seen quite often walking down the corridors and Jane Seymour seems only to appear on the anniversary of her son's death. The most dramatic vision, allegedly, is that of Katharine Howard. She is supposed

to run the full length of the haunted gallery and then to pound on the chapel door begging for mercy.

A lady in our development circle had a problem with an unwanted spirit of a man, who was in her house. He was appearing quite clearly to her son who would see and hear him and found him very frightening. He struggled to sleep at night because the spirit of this man was usually in his room. On New Year's Eve a few years ago, a party was held in the house. This resulted in the lady and her children all sleeping in her son's room, as the other rooms had guests in. The spirit of the man made his presence fully apparent to the lady concerned and was very intimidating towards her. She said that at the time he felt very aggressive towards her and he wanted her out of the room. His negativity towards her was overwhelming. This lady was quite a strong character; she felt annoyed with him even more so. She approached Jody, asking for her advice. Jody talked her through the same exercise that we had performed with Joe and Peter. This is explained below.

This exercise may seem a little unusual, but if and when you get called into someone's home, you will need to know what to do. Start off by talking to all of the people within the household who have experienced any activity, face to face. This is to ascertain exactly what has been happening and will give you a good idea as to what has been experienced by whom. It should also give you a good idea as to how much hysteria, if any, has been created. You can also read their body language and get a feel for what is being said to you. By being face to face you can tell if someone is genuine in what they are saying, or if they are stringing you along. You should be able to tell if they believe what has happened to be valid, or if it is purely made up. Go through the following checklist:

How much activity is being felt, or sensed? Is this hourly, daily, weekly, or just occasionally?

What exactly is happening or being felt? Is this heard, physically felt, or are objects moving?

Who is feeling the most activity? Is it mainly one person, or equal to all within the home?

Does it feel malevolent, malicious, or quite harmless?

Is the activity in one particular room, or rooms?

Do they know of any history behind why the home may be open to activity?

If there is one person who is sensing a lot of spiritual activity; do they sense spirits elsewhere, other than this place? They may be quite psychic/clairvoyant themselves and just need to know how to stop it. Children and pubescent teenagers are very sensitive to spirit and are often open to all sorts of activity.

Once you have gone through the checklist and have hopefully worked out if this is a genuine incident, you will need to go into the rooms in question to see what you are picking up on. As soon as you are in the room, find somewhere you can sit quietly for a moment and picture yourself surrounded in a bright white or pink light. Have your feet firmly flat on the floor and picture roots coming out of your feet so that you remain grounded. See if you can feel anything unusual. You should be able to sense straight away if there is something untoward happening, or simply feel the energy of the room. If it feels very negative, then there will be a reason why. It could be that either the main occupants have suffered from depression at some point, or that there have been a series of events that have left their 'mark' on the room. It could be that the room actually does have a spirit or two loitering around. For example, if a lot of abuse has happened within a house, then this will affect how the house feels. A good medium should be able to pick up on this. It may not necessarily be haunted, but instead it will have a bad vibe about the place. After a moment or two, ask if anyone would like to talk to you or deliver a message to another person. See what you sense or feel. This will be through the same sensations as you normally receive when in communication with spirit.

The message, if there is one, will be received by the same methods. If you find something significant happens, try to keep your cool as much as possible and listen to what is being said. It may be that you have occupants from way back who feel the house is theirs and they are really hacked off. Once you have made contact you will need to explain to them that the house is no longer theirs and that there is a much happier place they should be. Treat them like a living person if you struggle with what to say. Afterwards, you will need to guide them towards the light and help them cross over. Picture this in your mind. You will need to imagine a dark tunnel with a light at the end. Take their hand, or walk with them towards the light, letting them know that they are safe. It will be a much happier place to stay and there will be loved ones there who have missed them. Take them as far as you can and then let them walk the final part themselves, where loved ones and friends will be waiting.

To close a room down to unwanted activity, you need to picture a large, circular window on a wall within the room. Imagine you can see out to a beautiful sunny meadow full of wild flowers, with trees and hills in the distance. Begin to see the window shrink slowly, so that the view to the meadow gets smaller and smaller. Eventually picture it so tiny that it looks like a pin prick and then close it completely. Ask guardian angels to keep the room free from unwanted spirits and picture the room in bright white light. The room should feel a lot 'lighter' from negativity after this. Even if you do not sense anything much at all it still helps to 'cleanse' the room, mainly so that the people who are feeling the activity within the room are put at ease. Continue to do this in all of the other rooms necessary, but remember to picture your round window on an alternative wall to the one that you have previously used.

If you need to close a person to unwanted activity, then this can be done in a couple of ways. You can get them to perform a similar exercise to the one that you would undertake yourself. Have them sitting down with their feet flat on the ground. Ask them to imagine themselves surrounded by a big pink blanket, with either pink or white light, all around them. Then ask them to imagine roots coming out of their feet and growing into the ground so that they are firmly grounded. Once they have completed this, ask them to picture a white light coming out of the top of their head. Just like the window looking out onto the meadow, get them to picture the light becoming smaller and smaller until it's just a tiny dot, which finally closes over. This is a fabulous way of shutting out any negativity and also closing yourself down when you need a bit of peace and quiet. Hopefully, if they can follow this it should be quite effective.

Another way of shutting someone down is by closing their chakras for them, as mentioned in chapter 10. Many would argue that this process is mainly psychological for the person involved, but that's for them to decide. It does seem to work however and as long as it's effective, I'll continue using it. Ideally, have the person sitting down on a stool, or standing up, so you can place a hand either side of their body. You do not have to actually make physical contact if you prefer not to. Place both hands about an inch or two away from each chakra, starting at the crown. Imagine a light coming out from each chakra. Just as before, slowly feel the energy diminish and picture the light source getting smaller and smaller until it finally closes over. Then move on to the 6th brow chakra, or third eye. Place one hand in front of the body and the other hand behind the body, with the person themselves in the middle. When each of their chakras has been shut down ask for their guardian angels to watch over them and help stop any unwanted spirits from dropping in. Many mediums say a prayer to the Archangel Michael to ask for his protection against any negative entities. He is the leader of the archangels and a power to be reckoned with, particularly when low level entities are about. Apparently they will soon scarper if you bring in the heavy guns! We'll cover angels later on in the book.

Guidance Tips

I appreciate that this area of spirituality is going to be a difficult subject for some people, in that you will either love it or hate it! The idea of performing an exorcism or carrying out spiritual cleansing will put some people off completely. It's certainly not something all mediums do, so should you decide that this is not for you, then by all means stick to what you are comfortable doing.

When Jody asked if I wanted to go with her to a haunting, the idea at first took me by surprise and I wondered how I would cope with odd things flying around the room. Her advice ... Stay calm and try not to scream! Marvellous, I thought, this advice was meant to *help* me? I had visions of myself hiding behind Jody, or making a swift exit out of the door. The reality of this was actually a huge ghostly disappointment and not that exciting at all. To be honest, you will probably find this to be the same for you, too, should you get called upon. One hotel that we visited was, however, quite clearly haunted and a number of staff members had complained of seeing and feeling ghostly activity. The energy of the hotel was immensely different when we visited the older part of the building in comparison to the new part. As we viewed some of the rooms in which members of staff had seen or heard certain activity, I remember picking up on the feeling of a child being around. As we went into one room in particular, it felt like a little girl approximately 7years old had been there. Although we felt her energy around us, we didn't see anything and it certainly didn't feel uncomfortable or negative. This was quite different to how I imagined a haunted building to feel. I recall being very surprised at how comfortable I was with it and although I could feel her presence, it didn't feel negative at all. The staff that had seen this little girl were all quite scared, though. This was despite our best attempts to reassure them that in reality, she was totally harmless. There was a rumour of a little girl who died after falling out of one of the upstairs windows. This was before the house had become a hotel, but unfortunately no-one could verify this story. So, to this day we still don't know exactly what happened.

I think that when you know what you are dealing with, much of the fear is taken away. Most reported hauntings or spiritual activity is never as dramatic as most people think. Most castles, stately homes and older prisons, on the other hand, *will* most likely be haunted and there is little to be done to actually change that. As mentioned previously in the book, a haunting is like a recording of a tragic event, and no amount of 'cleansing' will help them towards the light. Technically there is no- one there to talk to, just the memory of the event which will usually have been quite tragic.

Jody has lived in a house where there has been a lot of spiritual activity that has been quite malevolent. She was young at the time and absolutely terrified. Light bulbs shattered, pictures kept falling off walls and children were often heard crying. The house they bought had been haunted for many years and had been sold for a ridiculously low price, which at the time they thought was a bargain. After putting out a plea on the radio for help, a medium came to live with them for 3-4 months, which helped to calm the activity until they could sell the house on. The medium picked up on Jody's ability to communicate with spirit and felt that this may have been a contributing factor. I think these instances are very rare and most spiritual activity can be dealt with without too much drama. If you do not feel happy doing a spiritual cleansing, then simply don't. Do not feel pressurised into anything that you are uncomfortable with; this is your journey and you can choose which path you take.

"In the main, ghosts are said to be forlorn and

generally miserable, if not downright depressed.

The jolly ghost is rare."

Dick Cavett

Chapter 12: Regression

If like me, you have seen various celebrities on TV claiming they were once living in Egypt or as a wise old man in a small English village, you may have thought that they were a sandwich or two short of a picnic! I have never been overly sure about this; although many people have described events and inhabitants with such clarity at times, it's hard to know what to believe. Jody described how our past lives usually have some bearing on our current lives. Therefore, if there was a lesson to be learned in a past life, we would come back in another life to correct it. For example, if in a previous life we had countless affairs and cheated on our partners, then we may find ourselves in our current lives as a person who is repeatedly cheated on. It's a trait that is often passed down through generations of family members. We may not, but it's possible. It may not necessarily be anything particularly dramatic, but something as simple as learning to overcome feelings of low self-esteem, or not allowing others to dominate us. I know this may seem to be an odd theory, but just go with it for now and read through this chapter. If after the exercise you still feel it's a bit too weird, then you certainly won't be the first. All I can say is try it and see what happens before you dismiss it. I was gob- smacked by what I saw as my past life. It was nothing like I had imagined and it did make perfect sense to me.

When we came into our development circle for a regression exercise, I had some major doubts as to whether or not this would actually work for me. I had no pre-conceived ideas at all and could not think for a minute where this would take me. I very much doubted for that matter, if I would get anything at all. Jody, when regressed, felt she was a soldier during the First World War who shot a young and innocent child, in addition to taking other lives. She felt that she had a total disregard for the lives she took and therefore her lesson in this life was to appreciate the lives of others. She had suffered multiple miscarriages, then, thankfully, was blessed with a son who is now a strapping young man. She felt she had to appreciate the importance of life and to not

131

take it for granted.

So as she talked about her past life, she explained to us that our past lives would also have some bearing on this life, too. We all sat there in anticipation of what we would sense in the way of a past life and some expressed how doubtful they were of getting any information at all. Jody then went on to explain that because we were going to look at a past life, or in fact a deep memory, the exercise was much easier than when we first met up with our spirit guides. We were told to give it a go and we would see what she was referring to by the end of the session. I will go through the meditation with you in the exercise a little later.

We all sat in a circle quietly and went through the meditation which involved going through a door. To begin with I found it a little difficult and achieved nothing. I then chose another door to go through and I was immediately transported to a foreign country. It looked like I was in a hot country, having a similar feel to that of Cairo or Jerusalem and I was immediately struck by how bright the sun was. I was looking down on a bustling market and there was red coloured sand and dust everywhere. The market had lots of people trading various foods, spices and different coloured woven blankets. I was a dark- skinned man wearing a coloured, striped robe and sandals and I had quite a full beard, which felt very odd to me! I felt as if I was in my late 50's, and although I was very dark- haired, I had a lot of grey coming through. As I walked through the market, most people seemed to know me and would wave or say hello. At one point several young children came running past me and tugged at the back of my robes before running off laughing. I knew that I was a familiar tradesman within this village; that was why people seemed to know me.

My mind then shifted to my home which was quite ample. It was clear that I didn't want for money, although I was not by any means excessively rich. I had a very young wife who looked to be at least 30 years younger than me. I also had two young sons, one around 12 years and the other about 10 years, plus one daughter who looked about 14 years old. I could tell that I absolutely idolised my sons and lavished praise and gifts on them; my daughter, however, was treated differently. I knew that I was extremely harsh with her and at times would beat her. My wife was also extremely submissive and I knew that our marriage was one that had been arranged. I felt that she didn't really fully love me, but fulfilled her duty as a wife and mother. Due to my financial status, the marriage had been deemed a 'wonderful honour' for her, but in fact this was mainly felt by her family. I felt she was not unhappy, but then not that happy either being my wife. She knew her place within the marriage, it was not an equal relationship. I didn't treat her as she treated me at all, in fact far from it; I made all of the decisions involving the home and family. She was there at my beck and call and was so submissive she dared not argue with me. My daughter, on the other hand, struggled to be submissive and was actually quite a feisty girl inside. She hated the fact that her brothers were allowed to do whatever they wanted and were actively encouraged to be dominant- the opposite to her. Looking at myself in this way, I quickly made the decision that I didn't like me at all and, in fact, felt quite disturbed that I would behave this way. I had little regard for women and felt that it was their duty to look after their men. Love, honour and obey me, was very much my ethic and I had no qualms about laying my hands on my wife or daughter if I felt this was not the case with them. What a charmer I was! My mind moved forward again and I could see how I died. I appeared to be being very sick with the most excruciating stomach pains. It looked a painful death, despite being quite short. From what I can gather, this was either caused by a very short and violent illness, or it was due to some form of accidental poisoning. Either way, it was not pleasant. Jody soon brought us all back and we slowly returned to our current reality. Nearly every person within our development circle had a clear experience from their regression. The funny thing was, not one of us turned out to have a past life that we expected. Each one of us could also see a correlation with the lives we were currently leading.

So, in my previous life, I had a clear disregard for women. If they didn't agree with my decisions or conform to my will, then I would beat them without guilt or hesitation. As far as I was concerned, the 'law' of my religion stated that this was how men were supposed to treat women and I was simply obeying that law. To me it was not wrong in any way, even though I could see the impact it was having on my family. My sons were being raised like little gods who could get away with anything and still enjoy their father's love. My wife, and particularly my daughter, only had to show the slightest amount of free will and I would literally knock it out of them. It therefore made sense to me that I would come back as a woman who was extremely feisty and constantly battled to be treated as independent; one who hates to rely on a man for anything!

My childhood consisted of men who treated women mostly as sexual objects, or who would sometimes lash out at them, particularly if the woman was a strong character and showed any signs of autonomy. For years I strived for a family and wanted to be the perfect wife and mother. All I wanted was a happy family home and yet when I actually got them, I felt frustrated and saddened. I felt that I should be doing much more with my life. It was only when I was in my late twenties that I felt I was finally doing something for myself. I went to college shortly after becoming a single parent and eventually went on to university. It was the exact opportunity I needed, as during my time at university I established that I did in fact have a brain! Furthermore, it seemed to work okay and I also learned to be independent. I would happily put up shelves, drill holes, mix concrete, etc. I even went on a brick- laying course, which was fabulous fun. I never wanted to rely on any man for anything and went so far in proving that I was self-reliant that I almost deliberately sabotaged any new relationship after three or four months. Any man who got too close to me was soon dropped like a hot potato! I found their expressions of love to be a sign of weakness, despite wanting to hear them initially. It really was the thrill of the chase. I craved excitement and wanted to be admired for my independence and my intellect, rather than for being a gentle and loving person. I would easily attract men who would find me different to many women, but then I would soon tire of them and move on. My family would often joke about how I was like a cat with a mouse. At first I enjoyed the game of playing with the mouse, only to squash it later when bored. Thankfully I found my second husband, who was different to most men. He showed me that I could love, be gentle, but also keep my independence. He taught me that it was okay to be myself. He showed me the *real* me, behind all of the barriers I had erected around myself and finally I began to settle. I still have a very strong independent streak and my lust for life's experiences have not yet been quenched. However, I know that my husband accepts this and lets me do whatever it is that I feel I have to do. Likewise I encourage him to follow his dreams and I let him know that he is totally loved, even though I am often distant from him. There are not many men like him in the world, so I count my blessings that I have someone who does not feel threatened by my independence or successes. He encourages, supports and loves me for me and likewise I do the same for him. We rarely argue, but instead enjoy the life we have together and ride through all of the good bits and bad bits as one. Okay, sentiment over! Hopefully you can see where I am going with this, though. I started out as a very different person from the one I am now and thankfully I worked out why that was.

Getting back to regression, another account of reincarnation stayed with me from way back in the 1980s. I was watching a programme about a young boy named Titu Singh, who was around 5 years old at the time the programme was made. From the age of four Titu absolutely insisted that he had lived previously in a village called Agra and that his name was, in fact, Suresh Verma. He had a wife, Uma, and two children. The boy, even though young, claimed his parents were not his parents at all. He suffered with severe depression, as he insisted he was a man of much older years, trapped in a young boy's body. He claimed to own a radio shop in a nearby village. He said that he had been shot in the head by two men, after he had arrived home one day in his car. He had been waiting for his wife to open the gate for him, when he was suddenly killed. His family were so worn down by his pleads to look into this for him that his older brother went to see if there was in fact a radio shop in the village of Agra. To his amazement there *was* a shop, just as Titu had said, and above it was a sign saying 'Suresh Radio Shop'. His brother went into the shop and asked to speak to Suresh, the owner, only to be told that he had died several years ago. The person suggested he speak to his widow, Uma. On meeting Uma, Titu's brother informed her that his little brother claimed to be her deceased husband. He said that Titu had described things about 'their' home life, which obviously came as a bit of a shock to her. Uma listened though and insisted on meeting Titu. She told the rest of her family about this little boy claiming to be her deceased husband. Suresh's parents and brothers were so amazed, they insisted on coming with her. When they met up and Titu saw Suresh's parents and wife, he was ecstatic and hugged them all. He drummed on a stool with his hands, as Suresh used to do previously as a child.

Suresh's family were obviously quite shocked and wanted to verify what this little boy was saying, so they took him to the village of Agra to visit the radio shop. They tried to mislead Titu and take him on a different road, but he showed them the way and shouted at them, 'Stop, this is where my shop is', when they tried to go past. He spoke with the family again, who were eventually convinced that this was evidently Suresh in Titu's body. His wife said that Titu had clearly recalled an event with her that only she knew about. He said that he had given her a particular bag of sweets on a picnic. Titu also had scars on his head, exactly where the bullet would have entered and exited Suresh's head. Titu, knowing the names of his murderers, gave these to his family who in turn informed the police. The man who had actually shot him was a businessman called Sedick Johaadien. When finally questioned by police, Sedick confessed to the murder.

There are many cases, such as this one, which are incredible to read about, but are also very difficult to dispute. I remember I was only around 12years or 13years of age when I first watched the documentary about Titu. To this day I can still picture the anguish and desperation showed by this little boy. He shed tears of frustration when interviewed because technically, to him, he was a fully grown man. He was reliant on his parents to take him everywhere, trapped in the body of a young boy. He was such a young boy and yet he spoke like an older man. It was incredible to watch and stuck with me for many years, as you can probably tell!

In our group regression, all of us saw events and lives that we had lived before. The strange thing is not one of us had any ideas about what sort of lives we would see. One lady saw herself as a blacksmith who would shoe horses. She had a wonderful wife and family and, from what she could tell, an idyllic life. Another was a young Victorian girl who lived in a large house in London with several members of her family. She could see herself looking down from an upstairs window onto the street below with horses and carriages going past. The family had plenty of money and servants, yet her life was far from happy. She eventually died a lonely woman, who never married or had children of her own. This caused some laughter within the group, as this lady now has four children and never has any time for herself! Quite the opposite in fact of what she saw happening in her past life. All of us were fascinated not only by what we saw, but also by how easy it was to see. It came quite effortlessly to most of us, despite our reservations, and we each had significantly different experiences.

Try working through this exercise and see what you feel. Make a note of the questions to ask yourself first, so that you can engineer your journey.

Try to find somewhere quiet where you won't be disturbed for a little while. Then work through this meditation, just like you have previously with others.

Sit or lay down somewhere so the energy can flow through you. If you are sitting down, make sure your feet are flat on the floor. Imagine roots coming out from your feet, so that you are grounded. Start by concentrating on your breathing. Breathe in deeply through your nose, then exhale fully. This can be back through the nose or through the mouth, then close your eyes. Lay your hands on your lap in an open position and concentrate on your breathing. Imagine a bright white light coming out from your abdomen and surrounding you in a large white glow.

Close your eyes and picture yourself standing at the bottom of a staircase with 10 steps and a door at the top. There is a lovely golden light coming from behind the door. As it feels warm and inviting, you are drawn towards the door. Concentrate on breathing deeply and slowly, then step up onto the first stair. You feel relaxed and safe as you continue to breathe deeply. Step up onto the second stair and notice how content and peaceful you feel. Still breathing deeply, you move up to the third stair and see the door clearly in front of you. Some letters are starting to appear on the door in gold writing, which spell out your name. Step forwards onto the fourth stair and see how your name is glowing brightly on the door in front of you. Move up again on to the fifth stair and breathe deeply, all of your stresses and strains of the day are gently drifting away as you step up again on to the sixth stair. You are feeling so relaxed now that nothing seems to bother you and you feel totally at ease.

Moving up again on to the seventh stair you feel very peaceful and unafraid; the door is in front of you and feels as if there is something wonderful behind it. Move up to the eighth stair and feel the light that is warm around you. It's stretching out from the door as you move up again on to the ninth stair. The door slowly begins to open and the golden light that comes out from the opening leaves you feeling calm and content. As you step up onto the last stair, the door opens fully onto a bright corridor, along which there are many doors. Each of the doors feels welcoming, nothing to fear and you then choose one to open. Go to this door and turn the handle. This door will open up on to a past life of yours. It's perfectly safe and nothing bad is going to happen to you. There is bright white light all around you and you feel quite calm and at ease looking at yourself in a previous life.

Are you male or female?

What age are you?

Where are you? Try to picture your surroundings and do not be afraid to look around.

What are you wearing and how do you feel?

What do you do in this life, what is your job?

Now move forward and picture your home.

What does your home look like?

Who is significant to you?

Are you married? What is your husband or wife like, are you happy together?

Do you have children? If so are they sons or daughters and what are their ages?

Do you have a happy life?

Do you suffer from any illnesses or ailments?

Do you have any animals around you?

Move forwards again and picture yourself towards the end of this life.

Have you had a contented life, or was it difficult?

How did you die in this life?

Was there anyone with you just before you died?

It's now time to come back, so picture the door in front of you and walk through it. You are now back in the corridor of doors, walking towards the stairs. The door leading onto the staircase is open and the corridor is full of bright, golden light. Slowly start to walk back down the staircase, taking each step slowly and breathing in deeply. You are feeling completely calm and relaxed as you near the bottom steps. Just as you get to the bottom you begin to slowly notice your surroundings, back in the room you are in. When you are ready, open your eyes once more. You will remain feeling totally safe and relaxed, as you become fully aware again.

Having pictured your past life, was there anything significant that stood out to you? Was there anything about your past life that you feel is significant to your life now? Do not worry if there was nothing that striking about the experience for you. It may be the case that your past life was quite run- of- the - mill. If we all visualised ourselves as Egyptian kings and queens I would be a little sceptical, to say the least. If I were to take a selection of approximately 20 people in a cafe, I would expect to have a mixture of backgrounds, occupations and experiences. This is exactly the same for past lives. Some would be wealthy and others poor, some would have had happy lives and others not. It would be just the same as taking a handful of people now; the only difference being that we have stepped back in time.

As mentioned earlier on in Chapter 2, I believe that we are all here to learn and it is *the* reason why we are all here in the first place. If you can look back on a past life and notice something that is significant to you, it may help you understand your current life. I am not saying for a second that people who have hard lives now were previously bad. I think if I did, I would be fetching the kindling and stake for myself! I just believe that we are here to learn and that sometimes our lessons may have come about from the lives we led previously.

I remember some time ago a chap appearing on TV, stating that all people with disabilities had been evil or cruel in a past life. To me this was utter rubbish then and still is now. I have two children of my own with learning disabilities, due to a form of autism. I am quite certain they were not evil murderers or bad people. Instead I feel that I have been blessed to have them. I can show them that despite their disability, they are still exceptional people who can overcome whatever life throws at them. They have taught me to fight against the stereotypical assumptions; that persons with learning disabilities should be treated differently and can never achieve as much as an able person. Parents should encourage their children to discover and work to their strengths, rather than accepting their disadvantages. They deserve just as much respect and love as any other person and I feel that maybe this will be part of their lesson. Their lesson is to learn that they are capable of success and happiness in their lives, too. Just because they have a disability it does not make them any less important or capable than anyone else. People need to learn to look at the spirit of the person inside the shell, not at the shell itself.

If you are looking a little glazed now, it probably means I've gone a bit too deep for you. Quite honestly, if I had heard someone say this to me 10 years ago, I would be sitting there feeling a little unsure if they possessed their full faculties, too! If it wasn't for the fact that I've experienced what I have experienced, I would say you were absolutely right to question them. When you go down the spiritual path, be prepared to take back some of your previous thoughts and notions. They have a habit of turning your world upside down.

Guidance Tips

If you find when you go through the meditation that you cannot see anything when you open the door, try another door. I found this myself the first time and looked upon a scene of 'nothing', which sent me into a small panic. So if this is the case for you, close the door you have just opened and then pick another. If after trying four or five doors you still get nothing, do not worry. It may be that this exercise is simply not for you, or that there are no past lives to look at. It may be the case that you are quite new to our Earthly plane. You may be a young soul that has yet to experience all the wonders that life has to throw your way.

If you do find that you can see onto a past life and are seeing things that you are not completely at ease with, then you can come out of this place and close the door behind you. Nothing bad is going to happen to you. We all have memories of events that were not the happiest in our lives and this may be the same. You have full control over what you do. If it turns out to be something that you do not feel particularly comfortable with, then come on out and close the door. Be aware of the room you are in again and picture yourself in a big pink blanket. Imagine the roots coming out from your feet and ground yourself, as you have done previously. It is a little odd I admit, but to be honest I didn't personally find regression uncomfortable at all, even when seeing my own demise. There was nothing fearful about the experience and in fact no-one in our group felt anything that made them anxious. I would be quite amazed if this were the case and certainly would not be suggesting that you undertake the exercise.

You may find that you have had a wonderful life and are quite happy having a nose around your previous habitat. Again this is perfectly safe, as long as you are quite content in your surroundings. You can always stay for a while longer if you choose, or come back another time. Make sure you go through the same meditation exercise beforehand.

You may find that if you enter through a different door on another occasion, you end up having a totally new experience. Do not be put off by this, as it will more than likely be that you have had other lives. So have a good peek around and see what you sense on another occasion. It may be that there is a recurring theme running through your experiences. This can mean that you probably didn't learn enough to graduate from the school of life and you have come back for another go at it. I know this sounds a bit nutty, but when you actually try this you will see what I am burbling on about. Well, I hope so anyway!

I have included regression as I feel a lot of people who come for readings do so when they are at their most vulnerable. They are looking to you for advice and hope. Quite often they may have had experiences in a past life that are repeated for generations at a time and it may be useful to try regressing them to see what their lessons in life are currently. I think it also has an impact on what sort of medium you will be, knowing where your ancestry lays. When you try it you should find that the images come through clearly like a distant memory and may prove quite enlightening for you.

"We are all visitors to this time, this place.

We are just passing through.

Our purpose here is to observe,

to learn, to grow, to love...

And then we return home."

Aboriginal quote – unknown author

Chapter 13: Animal Magic

Many people ask me what happens to their animals when they die and will they be waiting for them when they pass over? The answer is most definitely, yes. I have felt the presence of an animal that has come through quite clearly on a number of occasions. In the same way in which we sense the spirit of a person, mediums can describe an animal, too. They can state what the animal is, how it looks, how large it is and a little of its temperament. Just as people have souls that pass on, an animal's essence will also pass on. It is often cared for in spirit by a family member, or loved one, until such time that it can be joined with their owner again.

Being the owner of two dogs and a cat, I know I would immediately recognise my pets' temperaments, if they were described to me by someone else. One dog is small, grey and tan coloured, totally soppy, very gentle and a typical lap dog. She loves to be cuddled and made a fuss of. She is not the brightest of hounds and nothing much concerns her. She adores my husband and will always make a bee- line for him as soon as he sits down, although she will happily sit on anyone else who happens to be available, should he not be about. She also has a fetish for his socks! The other is small, white and beige, totally devoted to me and will follow me everywhere. She is the protector of the family and will herd my youngest son back to my side by barking at him, if he goes off course when out for a walk. My son is 15 years old, so it's not as if he is going to be at great risk if not glued to my side. Just try telling the dog that! She will bark and bark at him until he rejoins us and then she will merrily pad along beside us all. She often checks that the 'pack' is all together when out as a family and becomes quite distressed if we are not. I can go off by myself, but my children have their own furry bodyguard. As far as she is concerned Mum is pack leader and she is very obedient when with me. She is full of energy and will out- walk anyone. She is very intelligent, cunning and not much of a lap dog unless *she* chooses to be. She is pretty much the opposite of our other dog.

So you can see, as I've just written a whole paragraph on two dogs, it's quite easy to describe your pets. They are all very unique and totally different in look as well as in nature. Many people have heard their pets moving or padding about for weeks after their deaths. If an animal was loved and cared for, then they will know that they are missed and will want to drop back in to check their owners are okay. I think they will miss us just as much as we miss them in their own way, whatever breed of animal they are. Just because it's mainly cats and dogs that are seen in spirit form, does not mean that other animals do not have souls that pass on. I know many people who have become incredibly attached to iguanas, tortoises, rats and birds, to name but a few, and they too will all be waiting for us when we eventually pass on.

Our pets give us unconditional love and are often totally devoted to us. It's no surprise that we miss them just as much, if not more than a person, when they die. Pets are sometimes the only thing that keep some people going and are a huge comfort and support to their owners. How many animals have you heard that have rescued family members, whilst risking their own lives? Many pets will sense the mood and health of their owners. There have been countless times when I have been seriously ill or overwhelmingly sad, and found my dog right next to me, lying at my side. So many people have talked of similar accounts of their pet sensing their owner's pain. Their temperament changes to one of gentleness and compassion, as if they want their owner to feel better.

In the same way that we miss our pets when they die, they will equally feel our loss if we should die first. I am sure many of you are aware of the story of the Greyfriars Bobby, which has been dramatised several times. It's a true story of a gentleman, a policeman called John Gray, who had a watch dog who he named Bobby (very apt for a police dog). Bobby was a Skye terrier who was totally devoted to his owner and went everywhere with him for two years. When John Gray died of tuberculosis aged 43, the dog was found the next day sitting on top of the mound of earth which covered John's grave. Bobby was sent away by the curator of the cemetery as dogs were not allowed. However, the very next day Bobby was back on the mound again and so this continued. The curator, feeling sorry for the dog, brought him some food. The dog kept watch by John's grave every day in the Greyfriars cemetery for 14 years, until his own death in 1872, when he eventually joined his owner.

There is a granite fountain near the cemetery with a bronze statue of Bobby placed above it. It was sculpted from life and is sited on the pavement at the top of Candlemaker Row. This was created as a lasting memorial to Bobby, the little Skye terrier that had become a legend in his time. The inscription, which can still be seen, reads, "A tribute to the affectionate fidelity of Greyfriars Bobby. In 1858 this faithful dog followed the remains of his master to Greyfriars Churchyard and lingered near the spot until his death in 1872, with permission erected by Baroness Burdett-Coutts." The graves of both John Gray and Bobby his dog are in Edinburgh, in the Greyfriars cemetery. I cannot imagine for a moment that such a devoted dog would not be reunited with his owner. Just as our human loved ones pass over into the spirit world, our loved ones in animal form pass over there, too.

There are many animals that show great emotions. Some show emotions to such an extent that you could not imagine them *not* having souls. Elephants are fabulous examples of such sensitive animals. They show joy, pain and sadness, just like humans do. They show great signs of happiness amongst their family members and friends by playing games with them and also greeting them with vast displays of exuberance and excitement. They literally run towards each other, flapping their ears, rubbing tusks and trumpeting loudly when greeting a fellow elephant who has been absent for some time. How marvellous! They also show other emotions such as love, devotion, stress and grief, in a similar way to humans. One of the most moving demonstrations of emotion by elephants is during the grieving process. Years after a loved one has died, they will remain in mourning for them, often stopping quietly for several minutes at a place where the loved one died. They have been known to gently touch and handle the bones of the dead elephant and, whilst smelling the bones, they have been known to shed tears. How can such emotional and caring animals *not* have souls? I think due to these incredible characteristics elephants, and other amazing animals such as wolves and eagles, are often pictured as spirit animals or totems. They are revered by Native Americans and Shamans.

So let us have a look at some different animals and their characteristics, as they can play an important role in our clairvoyance. Animals can come to bring messages, or they can be representative in clairvoyance by their nature and habits. As I cannot mention every living animal, I can give some examples of animals that commonly crop up during dreams and clairvoyance, together with their general meanings. So take note if you sense or visualise an animal, as it may be a way that your guide is trying to communicate with you.

Apes – These animals are able to communicate very effectively through gesture and expression. They show compassion, intelligence, leadership and understanding. They can be associated with the need to connect with the inner child within us and also the need for us to use our imaginations for fun. They can be very good at problem solving and will show great strength and honour when required. Apes are a responsible and nurturing animal, often symbolizing the need to take action.

Bears - Many Native American cultures believe that the Great Spirit lives through the bear and that it's an animal of the mystics. The bear is highly protective of its young and at her most dangerous when protecting her cubs. They show enormous strength, but also are very nurturing. They are swift hunters of food, instinctively knowing when to be quiet and when to be active. Bears teach us that life's lessons can be harsh, but that we have the answers to the questions within us. They can be frightening and show a ferocious rage. However, underneath their fierce side is an animal that can be wounded just as easily as the next. They rely on their size and growl to protect themselves and place fear in others.

Cats – These animals have been associated with the spirit world for centuries. The Egyptians worshipped cats, often placing statues of them guarding the gateways to temples. They were thought to be in contact with spirits and protectors of the secrecies of the spirit world. They are typically indicative of independence, agility and free of will. Most cat owners will tell you that their cats will allow their owners to love them on their terms, not the other way round. They are extremely intuitive and playful. If seen as kittens during a reading, there will be a need for some 'playtime' within that person's life.

Deer or Stag – Majestic and beautiful, these creatures are alert and gentle. They symbolise a connection to the heart and soul, and although they will stand and fight when cornered, they would much prefer to run away. This can be representative of how a person tackles their own problems, by choosing to run from them unless there is no other alternative. They can also be inspirational creatures that invoke heartfelt emotions through gently steering the person to the answer, rather than pushing them into change.

Dogs – These are wonderfully loyal animals that love their owners unconditionally. They often sense danger or trouble very quickly and have a strong instinct to protect their pack. Now depending which breed of dog is pictured will illustrate their characteristics and the symbolism of the message. For example, terriers are tenacious little dogs that never give up, showing an incredible determination. Irish setters tend to be nervous and can crave attention at times. Labradors are playful and strong, not knowing their own strength on occasions. They are very much a family member who needs to be loved and included, very much like a child, in order to thrive. If unsure, try to find out the typical characteristics of the dog you are picturing or dreaming about and it should relate to the message you are being told.

Fox – Another animal that is regarded as sacred, foxes are often said to show the pathway to the spirit world. They are cunning and very clever; having an ability to move about quietly, swiftly and often unnoticed, they blend into their surroundings. They come out at dusk to do their hunting during the twilight hours until dawn, when they hide away again. Foxes can be indicative of the need to step back from a situation, to observe rather than launching head first into action. They often take a neutral stance when threatened, not wishing to become involved in a conflict.

Horses – Powerful and free spirited, horses can be hard to control. So depending on what the horse is doing, will depend on the meaning. If the horse is charging freely in the wild, it may mean a person's need for freedom and space. If the horse is quiet and still, it may indicate a strong ally or friend. Some people have seen horses nearby when connecting with their spirit guides, which would signify a strong protector and partner.

Mice – Despite its size, the mouse is a hard working little animal that stores food away in preparation for times when food is short. Easily frightened, the mouse can symbolise the desire to hold on to our fears, rather than face them. They often work away unnoticed and can become overlooked, not wanting to draw attention to themselves. This can emulate how many people feel during the course of their lives.

Pigs – Extremely intelligent animals, the pig shows great intuition and loves to have companionship. They are playful animals who will bask in the warm sunshine and they like to be in control of their own space. The pig can symbolise stubbornness, as they will tend to do what they want, but they also need to be able to trust others. They can also be great companions, believe it or not, and many pig owners will tell you how they each have their own characteristics that make them a good pet.

Rabbits – An animal known for living on its wits and for procreating wildly, the rabbit is often associated with hidden messages and quick thinking. In some cultures, rabbits are associated with good fortune, wisdom and guidance.

Wolves – One of the most representative animals of intuition and deep inner knowledge, the wolf is placed in the heart of the wilderness. They are instinctive and stay within the pack when possible. They will look out for each other and share a great understanding of the pack dynamics, which are essential for survival. They are symbolic of wisdom, intuition and determination, showing courage in life and death situations. Often they are seen during meditations and dreams, when a person begins their spiritual journey. They portray a desire for more spiritual knowledge and an acceptance of what is to come, despite the hardships.

<u>Exercise 13 – Animal Essence</u>

For those of you who have pets, or know someone who has a pet, this should be quite easy. For those of you who do not have a pet, you can choose an animal that you like, or you can leave this exercise out.

I would like you to do the same as I have above with my two dogs, and describe the essence of your pet, or one that is known to you. Think about their characteristics. Are they cheeky, dominant or gentle and how do they display these characteristics? If you were describing them to someone, what would you say? You do not need to note this down, but it is useful for being able to recognise when the spirit of an animal comes through. For example, when your pet has done something cheeky that they shouldn't have done, how do you know? You may find that someone's pet in spirit will give you the same images of your own pet. This is so you can recognise their character and can describe it to their owner.

Another way in which animals make their presence felt, are through dreams. Most of us have dreamt at some point in our lives about an animal, which is usually an indication of something significant. For example, if you think of a particular animal, such as a lion, what qualities would you associate with that of the lion? I would expect you to mention words such as: strength, power, bravery, imposing and proud. So if you have a particular dream about an animal, try to make notes of what happens. It's likely to have some relevance to you, or to something that is happening around you. Dreams, after all, are a series of images and symbols that are played out in our heads. This is by way of our subconscious self trying to make our conscious self aware of what is actually happening. If you have a recurring dream of an animal, then this can be analysed by looking at which animal it is. Analyse their qualities and what is happening within the dream and you should be able to interpret the meaning of it. Once the meaning has been established, most recurring dreams tend to stop.

Animals, I believe, come to us when a loved one has passed over and I have had personal experience of this. A medium said to me during a reading that my Dad kept showing butterflies around him. For his funeral, I wore a silk scarf covered in little butterflies and my handbag was also covered in butterflies. Since then, when I feel his presence, I often see butterflies at the same time. A friend of mine, who lost her son, sees feathers. Whenever she sees a feather on her back doorstep, she knows it's her son letting her know he's okay. So look out for our animal friends, as they are just as important in the spirit world and bring messages to us. Sometimes it's just a case of noticing them in dreams and meditations, then interpreting their meaning.

I have also seen animals come through during readings. I don't *see* them as such, but instead have the impression of the animal. One lady had sent me a photograph of her grandmother for me to read. I could pick up a lot of information about this lady from the photograph, and then when connected to her, I was aware of a small dog bouncing around her. Her dog, Molly, had passed over a little while before her and was happily with her in spirit. She was a very bouncy little dog that was clearly pleased to be reunited with her owner. I am also sure the lady was equally pleased to see Molly in return. I think it's fantastic when animals come through, as they would have given so much comfort to their owners when alive. I know that I would definitely want my dogs with me when I pass over. I'm quite sure that they will be looked after in spirit by someone in my family, until I am personally reunited   with them.

"Until one has loved an animal,

a part of one's soul remains unawakened."

Anatole France

Chapter 14: Angels

People often ask about angels and how to recognise when they are with us. Angels have been around for centuries and are often described in religious scriptures. In fact, the existence of angels is probably the one fact that most religions agree on, although they are often given different names, according to different cultures and religions. Angels are commonly referred to in the scriptures as God's messengers and were God's first creation, before anything else. They have never been human, despite being portrayed as chubby, winged, humanlike cherubs. These are the typical images shown on many greetings cards. They are said to be powerful, joyful, compassionate and loving beings that are here to guide and protect us for the good of God. This is obviously a very religious viewpoint. For those people who do not necessarily believe in God in the Biblical sense, this may not sit comfortably with you. I myself do not believe in God in the conventional way, but I definitely feel there are higher beings and angels that work alongside them.

I think that angels are around us, appearing just like any other person when necessary, to steer us in the right direction. I think they have a way of lending a helping hand (or wing) from time to time. I believe that we all have a guardian angel assigned to us, from the second we are created at conception, to our last breath when we die. They are here to guide, love and nurture us as much as possible, although I feel they have limitations as to what they can help us with. If they helped us with every aspect of our lives that causes us trouble, we would be back to the old argument of 'What's the point of life?' If you take the viewpoint that life is a lesson to be learned, then angels would obviously have boundaries. Some people say we each have one angel, others that we have numerous angels, or that one angel looks after several people. No-one knows which of these is actually true, if any. I personally am quite convinced that we do, at least, have a guardian angel designated to us.

There are plentiful accounts of people being visited by angels, but although no accounts can actually be proven, their existence appears to be accepted quite readily by many people. There are hundreds of stories of similar experiences, mainly by people who claimed to have been visited by a guardian angel, right at the time when they have been sad, grieving, in danger, or in need of inspiration. Most have described them as looking like ordinary people without wings, who have either vanished or melted away. Some have described family members as guardian angels who have dropped in when required, or they have just felt their presence. Personally I think all of these are accurate and that our family members, if close to us, would naturally want to look out for us, even when they have passed over. I know I would want to be around my loved ones and give them a gentle nudge, or a helping hand, whenever I could. Some people discuss the feeling of a rush of warm air going past them just before a disaster occurs. Many people say that they have heard angelic noises, or felt soft wings folding around them, in times of sadness. Others have had the feeling of comfort and warmth.

There have been many cases of near misses assigned to angels that usually come to light after large disasters or tragedies, such as earthquakes, floods, and acts of terrorism similar to 9/11. There was one case I saw on a television report, of a young Scottish girl who claimed she was next to a guardian angel when the shop she was working in blew up. It killed twenty two people and was due to a gas explosion. The young girl had been chatting in the basement with several colleagues, when she was called to tend to a lady. The woman asked her for an item that was in the shop's window display upstairs. As soon as the girl reached the window display, she felt a huge whoosh go past her, which was the explosion. It was caused by gas escaping out from the mains into an unventilated space below the shop. Had she stayed in the basement then she would have been killed, along with the two work colleagues she had been previously chatting to. The explosion left part of the building collapsed with thick smoke and debris littered everywhere, yet she was extremely lucky to come out unharmed. This was many years ago but she still claims to this day that the woman who asked her for an item from the shop window was her guardian angel and was never seen again after the event. There are numerous accounts like these that are always going to be difficult to prove. No-one will be able to provide actual evidence of guardian angels, not yet anyhow, but I feel quite comforted at the thought of someone looking out for me and being there when I need them.

Archangels are different to guardian angels in that they have more power available, a little like bringing in a SWAT team to resolve a problem. I am going to cover four archangels next, as I think they will have most relevance to your clairvoyance and may be of use to you throughout your spiritual journey. I have based my information on my own beliefs and also from what has been written, in both biblical texts and spiritual writings, all of which say very much the same thing. So at least most people who believe in angels are nearly all singing from the same song sheet!

A few angel facts: Archangels in Christianity/Hebrew each have names ending in 'el', meaning 'of God', and although it's agreed in the scriptures that God did in fact create the archangels, there is much debate about how many there are and who they all are. Depending on which religion the bible/ holy book is written for, will depend on which names crop up. For example, the Jewish faith has one opinion and The Old Testament has another, plus there are other religions, such as Islam, where the numbers of Archangels vary to what Christians believe. Michael, Gabriel, Uriel and Raphael tend to appear in many writings on the subject, and seem to be firm favourites. Although after this it gets a little tricky and it's up for much debate. Remiel, Raguel, Sariel, Barachiel, Metatron, and Raziel to name but a few, have all been mentioned as archangels, although only God knows how many Archangels there actually are! They, too, are here for our guidance and protection, but they can also invoke our creative and artistic side. From music, art and literature, to inner strength and calm, the archangels can give us a spiritual push when needed.

The first archangel is Michael, translated as – 'Who is like God', and he is the leader of all the archangels. He is often portrayed with a flaming sword and is responsible for protection, bravery, strength, truth and honesty. When he is around you may feel that you are in the company of the school's headmaster, or a senior policeman; someone you respect for their authority. Michael would be the archangel to call on if you found yourself being bothered by a lower level spirit, or if you feel that you lack commitment or motivation. He can give you courage, motivation and self-worth, in order to fulfil life's purpose. If you are struggling with life and experiencing inner turmoil, he would be the angel to call on for help. Tell him your troubles and ask for him to ease your worries.

Gabriel, translated as 'God is my strength', is said to be the angel concerned with conception, mercy, resurrection and death. It was Gabriel who foretold Mary that she was to have a child of God, to be named Jesus. Within many legends it has been said that Gabriel selects souls from heaven to be nurtured for nine months before birth. During those nine months Gabriel informs the child of all the things that he or she needs to know of Earth. He then silences the child before birth by gently pressing his finger onto the child's lips, producing a cleft above the lips and below the nose. I think this is a lovely tale and, if nothing else, it makes for an interesting read. Gabriel will help you discover your life's purpose and provide guidance on achieving this. He would be the one to call on if you were having difficulty with your spiritual vision. He is a calming influence and wonderful to talk to in times of stress or anxiety.

Raphael, translated as 'God has healed', is an archangel concerned with...yes you've guessed it, healing! He is a powerful healer of both humans and animals and is often called upon by those in the medical profession. He cannot interfere with a person's free will, so healing cannot be forced upon a person who does not want it. Raphael can help to heal both physical and emotional wounds. He comes across as gentle- natured and quite chatty when his presence is felt. Like Michael, he can often help to escort lower level entities away when they have outstayed their welcome. As well as having the power of healing, Raphael is the Patron Saint of Travellers and can be called upon for a safe journey.

Uriel, translated as 'God's light', is considered one of the wisest of the archangels and is said to give prophecies and warnings of severe weather and other natural disasters. He is often pictured with his hand held out, with a flame in his palm. Uriel is great for getting inspiration and for practical solutions to problems. If you want someone who can advise on how to build an ark when a flood may be coming, this chap is the one for you. Uriel has a passion for music and would be great for some melodic inspiration.

Using an example of asking archangels for help; I had a 40th birthday recently in which my husband and I went away for a weekend. We stayed in the most beautiful hotel, which dated back to the 17th century when it was first built. The hotel had the most fantastic spa and we merrily wallowed away in the aqua therapy pools. The spa had been created as a new addition to the old house. As soon as we came out of the spa and went into the old part of the hotel where our room was, the feel of the house changed drastically. It was beautiful and very tastefully furnished, but as we approached the main hallway where the main staircase was placed, the energy was very different. The energy was so different from the more modern building it was almost tangible; you could immediately tell that the hotel had some spiritual activity going on. My spiritual aerial was going mad and as we approached one room in particular, this intensified. My breathing became very short and I began to struggle for breath. I said to a very nice gentleman who was escorting us, 'Keith the concierge', that I felt the hotel was haunted, to which he said yes, it was. A lady named Alice had been murdered in the room we were approaching and the spirit of a priest had also been seen in the grounds. Although this didn't bother us in the slightest, we could both feel various spirits around. That evening after dinner, we went back to our room and collapsed into one of the most comfortable beds we'd had the pleasure of staying in for some time. We were both extremely tired and started to drift off to sleep. Just as I was drifting off I heard a whole heap of voices and sounds next to me. My husband had the duvet over his head at one point because he 'saw' a woman at the end of our bed. I could not see her though and started frantically looking around the room for this lady. Just as I was peering around, I heard a strangled rasping noise right next to me and felt that he may have had a point after all! For hours there was a constant array of noises and voices, so neither of us slept much. In the end I called upon Archangel Michael and my spirit guide to block out these unwanted guests; I then pictured my husband and I wrapped in a pink blanket of light. Within a few minutes we were both asleep and spent the remainder of the night undisturbed. We no longer heard or saw anything else during the rest of our stay, but it did cause some excitement at the time.

Exercise 14 – Communicating with Angels

Although most believers say that they have not seen an angel, there are certain things that can be done to feel their presence. I believe that they are more than willing to communicate with us in exactly the same way as spirits do. We just need to listen to them.

If you have a question you would like an answer to, you need to actually ask it. Saying out loud will help, then listen to the first message that pops into your head. If you ask a clear and concise question, it makes it easier to receive a clear and concise answer. Obviously if you ask a ridiculous question, you will probably get an equally ridiculous answer or no answer at all. If you prefer, write down your questions or your problems that you would like help with. Leave it for a day or so and hopefully you will get your answer. You should find that the answers present themselves to you and you will somehow know the right thing to do. Do not expect a handwritten reply, or for an angel to drop in for a cup of tea and a chat. It would be rather lovely if they did, but sadly they don't as a rule, so you may need to be patient. It's about listening to your inner voice and occasionally subtle signs will come your way. You do need to be aware though and open to recognising the signs.

Receiving messages from angels is very similar to mediumship. Working as a medium can be very challenging, because you, as the medium, are expected to pull a miracle out of the hat for each customer that comes your way. People are looking for proof that their friends or loved ones are actually with you. There is nothing worse than a client who is sitting opposite you with their arms folded, sending every negative thought your way. This can be the same for angels. If you are open to them and embrace the fact that they will help you, your connection will be better. If you talk to them asking for proof or for physical signs in order to believe they are with you, then I am afraid you will have a long wait. In the same way that we gravitate towards likeminded people, who make us feel happy and comfortable in their presence, angels will do the same with us. They love to be around harmonious energies, so bear this in mind. The more you can put in to developing a relationship with your guardian angel, the more you will get back in return.

Many people believe that calling their names several times can help to bring in a specific archangel, so this may be something that works for you. I personally chat away openly if I need some assistance of guidance, although if someone is nearby I tend to do this mentally, rather than out loud, for obvious reasons.

"You'll meet more angels on a winding path

than on a straight one."

Terri Guillemets

Chapter 15: A Happy Medium

As mentioned previously, a medium with a huge amount of worries and problems in their life will possibly struggle to get clear information. They will not be in a good position to work with grieving people. Therefore it's crucial to take time out and also be true to yourself. If you are letting your family work you like a slave, then you are probably not doing yourself, or them, any favours. You need to be firmer with yourself and not just them. A happy medium is a good medium, despite all of the troubles that they have previously experienced. Do not carry your baggage around like a millstone! Put it in a 'box' and get rid of it so you can move on. If you treat it as an experience that you have learnt from, it's easier to help others who are going through a similar experience.

I recently had a great example of this when I met a lady who'd had a very poor upbringing. She'd had abusive parents who showed her little love. This lady carried so much hurt with her that she would try and block out those feelings with alcohol and would not let anyone get close enough to her to hurt her again. As a result of this she was actually hurting her own children in return, despite having much love for them. This is very easy to do. When we are hurt, we put up emotional barriers and quite often have relationships that end badly. You may even find that your choice of partner is exactly the same as the parent that hurt you, or the exact opposite to them, but with *you* emulating the parent's behaviour. The bottom line, though, is that you do not need to do this. Once you have come to terms with any issues and start appreciating yourself, you will find others will appreciate you in the same way.

Some time ago, about 20 years or so, I met a lady who was young, beautiful and in a very happy marriage. She seemed to have everything she wanted; her parents adored her and were very stable, she was someone who always had money and who enjoyed her life immensely. I would call this lady 'blessed'. I recall thinking how different her life was from mine and that I would never be that happy or fortunate. My upbringing was far from idyllic, in fact at times it was an extremely steep learning curve, but I muddled my way through and carried all of my issues around with me. It was not nice, but it was familiar and at times I craved what was familiar to me, regardless of whether or not it was right. My first husband did his best to support me, but I was what I would call 'a little damaged' and could not be fixed. I had various issues that I had not dealt with and could not understand why certain things had happened during my life.

When I look back at this younger me, I could give myself a good slap. Part of me thinks now, however, that I would not be the person I am now without those painful experiences. So maybe this was all part of the bigger plan. If you saw me now, you would have no idea of the background I came from. You would see a well presented and confident woman who adores her family and, on occasions, has an inner wisdom that the Dalai Lama would be proud of! I still run round like a headless chicken and despair of certain things, but anyone else would not be aware of this. Many think I have come from a lovely middle class background with very few concerns throughout my life, but the truth is far different. I have worked very hard to get over my issues and not let them dictate how I live now. The same can be said for many mediums; you would never attribute them with having such tragic life events, but many of them have. I truly believe it's those difficult and painful events that make us better at what we do. As spirit use our memory bank of feelings and images, it makes sense that we would be better 'readers' if we have experienced painful aspects of our lives, in order to be able to relate to others. A lot of mediumship involves working with people who are hurting or grieving, so if you have not experienced grief yourself, how could you relate to it?

I have, over the years, looked back at my past, and came to the decision about three years ago that carrying my box full of issues around with me was not doing me any good whatsoever, so I decided to get rid of it. I don't deny my experiences ever happened, but instead I eventually chose to learn from them. I was going to make sure that my children didn't go through a similar childhood. This is something I think we should all do, but it has to be a conscious decision. It's definitely not an easy task. Get rid of your old box of hurt feelings and emotions. As far as I am concerned you should burn the damn thing! Surround yourself in the new emotions that you both want and, quite frankly, deserve. Do something good for you and everyone around you will benefit, too. If you become a positive and happy person, then your family will see that as well. They will learn that despite all of the rubbish that happened to you, you can still be a happy person. You *can* overcome all of life's obstacles. Nothing is unconquerable; if you go through your life with that attitude, you will see how much better it is. By carrying around all of our emotional baggage, we hurt the ones we love. I have seen so many people who have been abused or badly hurt by their parents in the past. They carry their hurt like a medal, almost taking comfort in having something to hide behind. They say to me "I only drink/ take drugs/ shout at my children/ have numerous partners/ crave attention/ hurt my family/ steal (the list is endless), because of how I was brought up". This is absolutely right, it is because of how they were brought up, *but* they do not have to live like a wounded animal. If you wear your wounds like a medal, you may feel that this justifies how you behave now. It doesn't! You may find yourself turning into precisely the person you never wanted to be and your children may end up going down exactly the same route as you have. Remember, it's your life and you are in control of it. If you do not like part of it, then the only person stopping you from fixing it, is you. All I will say is that if I can change my life, then there really is nothing stopping you, too.

I am a big believer in the motto 'you get out of life exactly what you put in', so if you tell yourself that you will never do something great or never be someone positive, then you won't. For those who are familiar with it, there was a cult British TV series called Red Dwarf that was prevalent in the early nineties. It was based around two main characters that were trapped in deep space together. Unfortunately, they both had a great dislike for each other. One is the last surviving human, the other a hologram of his dead bunk mate. There are a few other characters in the space craft and they have various adventures trying to get back to Earth. I used to watch it avidly when it was on.

One of the episodes was called *'Better Than Life'*, in which each character was plugged into a game. The game plugged into their psyche and they each felt as if they were living out their deepest desires and dreams. This was great for most of the characters, except one, 'Arnold Rimmer'. He was unable to accept anything good happening to him and his neurotic mind took over, causing much havoc. Although he seemed to want good things and felt that he deserved them, as soon as he actually got what he wanted, it all went wrong. The problem for him was that deep down, he actually didn't feel as though he deserved anything good and he disliked himself. The game picked up on this inner fear and self-loathing and therefore gave him exactly what he subconsciously desired. No matter how hard he tried, everything that started out as good went horribly wrong. He really didn't like himself much because he had so many issues he hadn't dealt with. The other characters had quite simple lives and were very happy, right up until Arnold's disturbed mind infiltrated their lives. A whole book was written by Rob Grant and Doug Naylor, who also wrote the series Red Dwarf, which was extremely funny. The sad thing is this story applies to many of us. This is possibly why it was known as one of the most memorable episodes in the series.

When you truly start to believe in yourself and believe that good things will happen to you, then they will. We attract exactly what we think we are worth, so if you are in a mundane job or a poor relationship, it's probably because deep down you think it's all you are capable of, or deserve. In order to change this, we have to start to change how we view ourselves and believe that we deserve to be happy. You do not need to launch head first into a complete overhaul of your life, but start by taking those first steps to improve yourself. You attract in others exactly what you put out for them to see.

Exercise 15 – Paving the Way to Happiness

Here's what I would like you to do for your own happiness – try one of these every day and you will start to reap the benefits. It's very simple and doesn't take too much effort.

Power Shower – When you next leap into the shower, close your eyes and picture the water falling on you in colour. Choose a colour that seems right to you - going back to our colour theory in Chapter 4. If you would like to bring in more passion, go for a deep red or scarlet. If you would like to feel happier, go for a bright yellow or gold. For a more spiritual feeling, picture the water in a purple or lilac. For a healing colour possibly choose a blue or green, whichever feels right to you. As the water touches the top of your head, imagine this coloured water washing away all that is negative. Replace it with the positive feeling or emotion that you would like. You may find that your head becomes very sensitive, and the water leaves it tingling. Either way, you should come out feeling refreshed, clean and more positive than when you went in.

Focus Wheel – I know lots of people who use focus wheels to keep them focused on what makes them feel good or happy within their lives. I think they're great for actually noting down what it is that makes you happy because it can be hard to know until you actually think about it! A focus wheel literally looks like a wheel with a round centre and compartments in between the spokes coming out from the centre. Start by placing yourself in the centre, then list all of your good qualities in between the spokes. Put it up somewhere for you to see every day. These are also good if you want to actually focus on achieving something such as losing weight, getting a qualification, or giving up smoking, for example. Using a similar principle, write down what it is you want to achieve in the centre of the wheel and then list around the outside what benefits you will gain from achieving your goal. For example, if you want to gain a qualification, put that down in the centre of the wheel. Around the spokes you may write: I will gain self-confidence, I will be able to apply for the job I want, I can earn better money, with more money I can go on holiday, and so on. By focusing on what you want, you will find yourself more motivated as you see your target as a constant reminder.

In the sunshine – This seems a little obvious, but getting outside when the sun is shining will actually make you feel great. The reason for this is that sunlight increases your serotonin levels. This is a hormone released in your body that makes you feel good. Many antidepressants work on this hormone by making it stay in your blood stream for longer. Many people tend to get more depressed in winter months when the days are shorter. Some suffer from a condition called SAD, or Seasonal Affective Disorder, which is caused by a lack of sunshine. So if the sun is shining, even if it's a little cold, get outside for a short while and take in your surroundings, or just people- watch. It can be fun guessing the career of a person, or where they are dashing off to at that moment.

Something Creative – Some people are very artistic and have that ability to draw, paint, or do something creative. Even if you feel you are not one of these fortunate people, it's actually quite good fun to have a go. For those of you who have had young children about, you will know exactly what I mean. When you have had little ones about and have brought out the paints, glitter, glue, etc, you may have had one of those moments where you have had a go yourself, and thought 'actually this is quite good fun!' I had one of those a little while ago whilst looking after my friend's little boy, who was aged 5 at the time. It was coming up to Christmas, so we decided to make him a crown complete with glitter, buttons and painted pasta; in fact anything we could lay our hands on. We both enjoyed it thoroughly and had a great time painting and getting messy together. It struck me that as adults we feel we need an excuse to get the paints out, but it can be a great way of having fun. Try it yourself and you will see what I mean. You do not need to do potato prints or finger painting to bring out the inner child, there are lots of grown up ways to have fun and be creative.

Inner Child – Do something fun with the family or with some friends which you can all enjoy doing and do not be put off if you've never done it before. Jody and her family went ice skating recently, something she had not done for years and they all had great fun. They were in hysterics at her total inability to glide around the rink, whilst her brother and son went shooting round having the time of their lives. My husband and I hired a rowing boat one sunny day last year and went out on the river with the family. Even the dog joined us, although she did end up diving in the water at one point and had to be fished out! We had immense fun together and both of my boys talk about that day very fondly, even now. They recently asked if we can all do it again this summer. There are lots of other things you can do to bring out the fun side in you. Let your inhibitions go and think like a child again. Get your wellies out and go wading in puddles or paddling in the sea. The more in touch you are with your fun side, the more you will begin to enjoy life. Sometimes it's the silly little things that really make us smile.

A Random Act of Kindness – This one can be very rewarding, especially if the person is not expecting it. It involves doing something kind or thoughtful for someone when they have not asked you to. One lady, who goes into a coffee shop near me, always pays for a cup of coffee for the person behind her in the queue. It's not a huge thing, but it's always much appreciated by the person who receives the kind gesture. I once saw a man carrying a petrol can as he walked down the road in the pouring rain. He was with his son who must have been about 9 years old. The petrol station was a good half an hour's walk away and I was driving home at the time. I recall turning the car around and offering to drive the man to the petrol station and back to his car, which he gladly accepted. This was not the sort of thing I would normally do, but as the man had his son with him, I felt so sorry for both of them trudging along in the rain that I offered to drive them. It only took 10 minutes out of my day, but I knew that he and his son were very thankful. They were on holiday in the town and had run out of fuel due to a faulty petrol gauge. The man said that he thought the fuel was low in the car but had not realised how low it was until he had run out. Again, it was not a big deal to me, but it certainly helped them out. So do something nice for someone. It doesn't have to be for a total stranger; it can be for your partner or a friend just a gesture to say' I thought of you today'.

If you can do something that actually makes you smile or feel good about yourself, then do it. I think we are often our own worst critics and spend a lot of time and energy chastising ourselves, when we could in fact be doing something far more constructive. The more positive you are and stand up for what you truly believe is right, then the more you will thrive in life. We all go through bad and painful periods in our lives, but if we believe in ourselves and have good relationships with our friends and families, we are more likely to get over them. I have a lovely quotation that I often refer to when I feel a bit sorry for myself.

During mighty storms the trees that survive

are those with the strongest roots.

They get shaken, but they stand.

Chapter 16: Coming Out of the Closet

Well, congratulations to you if you have come to the end of this and feel that you are finally getting to where you want to be! I can recall the exact moment when I decided that this was 'it'. I was tired of hiding away and wanted to put my new- found skills to work. I knew that telling my family was going to be the hardest part of my new career and that some of them would be quite bemused at my choice of work. This was always going to be hard and to be completely fair, there is no easy way of coming out. It feels like admitting you are gay to a homophobic parent. The typical stereotypes and assumptions are made and some people will be too embarrassed to discuss your work. Personally, I think that if it feels right, then do it. Being a repressed medium is not going to do you any favours. You do not have to tell everyone all at once, but you have to start somewhere. Most mediums work by giving readings and these tend to come about through word of mouth, so it's a bit difficult to keep quiet.

It's hard to be able to gain experience and practice if you are not yet 'out of the closet', as you need new people to read for. In order to gain experience, you have to finally come out and announce to the world that you are now a practicing medium. Or in other words, tell a few close friends and hope they spread the word for you.

Several of us in our development circle felt as if we wanted to spread our wings and finally take flight. Like any new profession, you are not going to excel at this within a few months of coming out. It takes time and practise to fully appreciate and trust the information you receive. The more you work with your gift, the better you will become. Treat it like any new job. It may be that you decide you would rather stay hidden from the world and not do anything with your abilities, or it may be that you decide to do the odd reading now and then, which is also fine. You must do what you feel is right for you!

If, on the other hand, you feel you want to spread your wings, too, there are several ways in which to go about this and there are a few things you can do to help develop your confidence. An absolute must is to go and see other mediums at work as you will be able to observe how others go about their profession. Some will be mainly using their psychic skills, using Tarot cards or such like, others will be mainly clairvoyant, giving their information as it comes through. If you go and see a leading clairvoyant you will notice how they get their information and stick with it. They will be confident enough to know that the information they receive is accurate and will not retract it. If you then see a poor example you will probably notice how they change the information to 'fit' the person. It may be quite convincing and the person involved may appear to be quite happy with the message. If the medium continues to work this way, I would be extremely wary. There are many con- artists who are clever at convincing people that they are mediums, simply by looking at the person's body language and reactions. They have learned how to trick people into believing them and are giving messages the person wants to hear, playing on an individual's grief. It's always good to observe both good and bad practicing mediums so you know what you are up against. Try to see why a particular medium is considered good. Have a look on You Tube if you have access to it and you will be able to see a whole host of various mediums in action.

If you have some friends who know of your new ability, ask them to put the word out for you that you are doing readings for people. Normally when this happens, you find yourself with an influx of willing people to practise on. So many people are curious about clairvoyance that it shouldn't be too difficult to find someone to read for; preferably someone you have not met before. Remind them that you are practising and do not charge for your time, unless you are confident that you can deliver a *good* reading.

Some ladies in our development circle decided to get together and invite some friends round for a psychic evening. There were four of them practising their clairvoyance; some used Tarot cards and others didn't and each brought two or more friends with them. It was a little daunting to begin with, but each of them did a fabulous job once they got over their initial nerves. They all read for someone that they had no previous knowledge of and this gave them the confirmation that their information was accurate. So if this is a possibility for you, it's quite a nice way to start off gently.

Make sure that you give yourself thinking time and not hurry yourself, as this can have a big effect on your nerves. I decided after delivering some accurate readings that I wanted to project myself forward and become more involved. Jody had been holding clairvoyant evenings for many years. These were at various venues where she would deliver messages to a host of people. Although I had never seen her at work, we both felt that I was ready to do the same as I was picking up on spirits quite easily when I connected. We both discussed this and arranged an evening at a local spiritual church. We were both quite excited about my 'debut' night.

Our first night at the spiritualist church brought in about 40 people or more. The whole venue was full to the brim and I sat at the front with Jody, getting my connections whilst a reading was being given. As I sat there I could feel that there was a lady in spirit with a gentleman near the front and another lady in spirit, who was with a gentleman near the back. Jody told me that this connection was as good as any to start with and that once I started to talk the information would come. Jody gave a whole range of fantastic readings for people and her information came out thick and fast. She was like a freight train pounding along; it was totally incredible! Then the time came for me to stand up, so I introduced myself and felt quite confident as I began to describe the lady in spirit I felt with the gentleman near the front. This turned out to be Mum - in- law, so I began to give the information I was receiving. It was a lot slower than Jody's but still accurate. As this man's wife was there, I spoke to her, too, but felt I should wrap things up after 5 minutes or so. I was too keen to show my new ability and move on to another person as Jody had done. I also kept hearing the name 'Jean ', but was too nervous of saying the name in case it was wrong. Although I could have kept going I didn't and yet I should have. The connection was good and the information probably would have continued to flow, but I was too worried about spending a long time with one person when the information was coming out slowly. I then moved onto my other gentleman and started describing the spirit of what I felt was his wife. It started off okay and then I felt myself start to clam up a little, when I asked if they had three daughters. He said, 'no, there were only two daughters and a son'. I checked my information again and had a strong feeling of three girls and a son, but apologised to him for getting it wrong. The more I continued, the more I panicked, and then felt too afraid to say what I thought. I was like a rabbit caught in headlights and I almost completely froze. I handed back over to Jody who was able to pick up where I had paused and off she launched again. It turned out the man had another daughter *in spirit*, but not living. I was so mad with myself. I sat back feeling absolutely awful knowing that I had allowed myself to panic, almost shutting out any information I received. All of my basic rules went straight out of the window, and I was cursing myself for thinking that I was ready. Jody had been doing this for over 20 years and here was I all full of confidence after five months of 'coming out'. My logical head was thinking that if it was easy in a development circle, then it would be easy here.

We both had a good long chat after the event, in which Jody said she would not have even thought about going 'public' after five months. I was also told that the first lady I read had a sister who was 'hiding' at the back. She was very skeptical and did not want to give anything away by sitting with her family member and yes, her name was Jean. Maybe I was trying to run before I could walk and this was the lesson I needed. Jody sat me down to watch 'YouTube' so that I could see other mediums at work; those who were good and those who were not. I slowly began to realise that maybe I was trying too hard. Most of them were much slower than Jody and also took their time. Most didn't give names or ages, but instead discussed the emotions associated with the person, as I had done previously in circle. I was so annoyed with myself for trying to work in the same way as Jody that every bit of confidence ebbed away from me and I knew that I needed to pick myself up again. Although I watched other mediums that worked in a very similar way to me, I knew that I needed to re-affirm my own abilities. Thankfully two lovely ladies came for a reading, armed with photographs of those they wanted to bring through. This worked wonderfully well for me and the information came through very clearly. I felt back on form again.

After this, a decision was made that I would stick to personal readings and I now do one or two every day. Mainly I work from photographs that are e-mailed to me if the person cannot visit me themselves. Since this decision was made and the pressure was taken off me, my mediumship skills have blossomed again. Each month I notice that I find out something new. On a one- to- one basis I find the information just flows, but it's not always easy. Some readings I have had to work hard for. I find those who are more recently bereaved or who are grieving a lot, are much easier to read for than those who have long come to terms with their grief. I think spirit connects with me most clearly when I am most needed. When you have someone sitting in front of you with their arms crossed wanting solid evidence, it's harder to make a good connection. The more open someone is, the better the reading will be as spirit will want to communicate. If a person does not really believe in anything you say, even when it's accurate, then spirit will most likely not feel inclined to communicate with them. Imagine how you would feel if it was you in spirit trying to talk to a relative of yours and they discredited everything you were passing to the medium and ignored your message! I am sure you would feel pretty fed up after a short while and not bother. This is exactly what it feels like for a medium when they encounter such a negative reception. It often feels like pulling teeth when working with a closed person! You have to constantly keep asking for information from spirit which does not come through easily, whereas a person who engages with the medium has a much better reading. Spirit knows that they are able to pass their message across and so give a lot more information; it just seems to flow. When mediumship is most needed or when someone is very open to receiving a message, it feels almost effortless and it flows beautifully. When you try this yourself you will see what I mean; you will find some connections just click for you and others don't.

Do not be afraid to learn as you go along; each time I do a reading I am very aware of my body language and the sensations I feel. Even now I am still finding new ones. If you are feeling something then tell the person or describe how you feel, as I can guarantee it will be relevant. You will find yourself a little wary of saying what you feel to begin with when you start seeing new people and it will take time. This is all quite normal. The other thing I found quite surprising is that people expect you to know everything and have all of the answers to solve their problems. Many will want to know about various issues, such as if their partner is right for them, will their children move abroad or be successful and will their finances be resolved? It's very difficult to say that you cannot tell, particularly when they are clinging on to your every word with hope. Please do not be tempted to do this, if this is not what you feel is right. You are practising your clairvoyant skills, not your predictive skills. The main part of clairvoyance is to reconnect people with loved ones who have passed on, not predict the future. If you make this clear at the beginning of a reading, it will save a lot of awkwardness and disappointment. Do not be afraid to say what you will and won't do during a reading. It's not for us to say what a person should or should not do with their lives. Carefully structured guidance is good, but in some cases you may need to recommend a counsellor or doctor. Some people have issues, or health problems which are far beyond the skills of a medium. Bear this in mind and try not to take on too much if it doesn't feel right. You will end up feeling drained yourself and find your own health going downhill.

<u>Exercise 16 – Diary</u>

Most people tend to groan at the thought of keeping a diary, but it makes your journey much easier and clearer to evaluate. It doesn't have to be a long - winded affair, with reams of writing each and every day, just a few lines will do. If that is too much then a smiley face will suffice! When you look back over the good days you have had, it certainly makes you feel better. Also make a note of any new experiences you are having, as over time you may make more sense of them. As you progress on your journey you will be aware that you are changing quite dramatically. It's only over time that you actually realise the extent of these changes.

If you make a note of the days that you have performed well, or had a positive experience, it really helps. Likewise, make a note of the days where you have struggled with a reading or felt your psychic switch turn off. When you look back you may find that the times when your spiritual aerial had not had a good connection were days when you had a lot on your mind, or were very busy. Spirit knows when we are at our best and will only give us what we are capable of working with. In my early days I found that my spiritual growth was blossoming rapidly and information came flooding in.

When I finally decided to make a career out of it, I felt my spiritual development slow down to a trickle, which was immensely frustrating. Many mediums will talk about quiet spells, where they have struggled to bring through spirit, or times when they felt they were not quite up to scratch. This is very worrying, but not unusual. By making a note in a diary of the times that you feel this, you may find that there is a very good reason for it. Once life has calmed down, you should be back in the driving seat, hurtling down the spiritual highway. Even if we want contact from spirit, we may not get it if the powers that be have decided that we are not ready, or need a little time out. If they could put this in writing a few weeks before it happens, this would be wonderful, but unfortunately they do not tend to give you any notice. It just happens! Clairvoyance is not an easy path, but it can be extremely rewarding. Personally, I think that providing proof that there is an afterlife and helping grieving people is priceless, so never underestimate how valuable and comforting that is.

You may notice changes in yourself when you progress further down the spiritual pathway; these are perfectly normal and something that most clairvoyant and spiritual people experience. These are:

- A feeling of being removed from the day to day worries and that life has a bigger purpose for you.
- Being less tolerant of friends and family who are quite 'needy' and those who worry about issues that seem trivial to you.
- A deeper appreciation of nature and the beauty within.
- Being less tolerant to alcohol and suffering from headaches and hangover- like symptoms after drinking only a little alcohol.
- Eating less unhealthy food and wanting to look after your body more.
- Wanting to remove yourself from the unkindness of others and be with likeminded people.
- Having an inner peace and a trust that life will work out for you.
- Feeling as if life is a lesson to learn, before going 'home'.
- A passion for more spiritual knowledge and wanting to progress.
- Being more sensitive and aware of your body and surroundings.
- A craving for chocolate after connecting to spirit!

So here we are at the end of my journey so far and hopefully at the beginning of yours. This was never a book meant to dictate how to learn clairvoyance and push spirituality, but instead give you more of a gentle nudge in the right direction and teach you not to be afraid of getting it wrong when you are learning. As you can see, I tried all sorts of different skills before finding which ones worked for me and most definitely got it wrong at times! Try different methods and see what works best for you. You can always dismiss those methods that do not work for you and come back to those that do. I can absolutely guarantee that the more you practise, the more you will learn and the better you will be. Trust your own instincts, as they will serve you best, certainly more than any book telling you what you should be feeling.

I hope you have taken something from this, even if it has been just food for thought, or maybe it will be the nudge you have been waiting for. Thank you for reading about my journey in learning how to communicate with the spirit world. I hope that you have found it enlightening and maybe a little different from what you expected.

Good luck with your own journey and remember - the greatest mistake you can make in life is to be continually afraid that you will make one!

Amy x

If you have taken anything from this book and found it useful, I would be extremely grateful if you could leave me a review on Amazon or anywhere you have bought this from. Reviews are what most people rely on to make an informed decision about purchasing and reading a book, so anything positive is always hugely appreciated!

Please note that all of the names within this book have been changed to protect the identities of the people concerned. I have not changed the name of Paul Derrick, the medium mentioned in the beginning of the book, who gave me my first ever reading. Instead I would like to thank him for the comfort he gave me and for instigating my fascination with clairvoyance.

Paul can be contacted on-line via: www.paulspiritmedium.co.uk

Reference List:

Farmer, S. D. Phd. (2010) *Earth Magic Oracle Cards Book.* London: Hay House Inc.

Guiley, R. E. (1991) *Harper's Encyclopedia of Mystical & Paranormal Experience.* San Francisco: Harper Collins.

Kilham, C. (2010) *Cocoa, The Health Miracle [online].* http://www.medicinehunter.com/cocoa-health-miracle. (Accessed 15th January 2012)

Mavromatis, A. (1987) *Hypnogogia: The Unique State of Consciousness Between Wakefulness and Sleep.* London: Routledge.

Oxford Dictionaries. (2011) *Concise Oxford English Dictionary: Main Edition.* Oxford: Oxford University Press.

Wood, D., *et al.* (2009) *History Features [online].* http://www.bbc.co.uk/gloucestershire/content/articles/2005/06/29/ley _lines_feature.shtml (Accessed 9th November 2011)